EXPLODING POPULATION MYTHS

JIM PERON

Foreword by Julian Simon

The Heartland Institute • USA

The Free Market Foundation • South Africa

EXPLODING
POPULATION
MYTHS

The views expressed are those of the author. Nothing here should be construed as reflecting the views of The Free Market Foundation or The Heartland Institute or as an attempt to aid or hinder the passage of any legislation.

Published by:

The Free Market Foundation
PO Box 785121
Sandton 2146
Johannesburg, South Africa
Tel: 27-11-884-0270

The Heartland Institute
800 East Northwest Highway Suite 1080
Palatine, Illinois 60067
United States
Tel: 708-202-3060

Cover photograph supplied by Anka Agency International

FMF Books ISBN 1-874-930-10-4
Heartland ISBN 0-9632027-4-X

This monograph has also been published in Canada by the Fraser Institute of Vancouver in a different format.

CONTENTS

FOREWORD
Julian L. Simon

Please note well Jim Peron's statements in his Personal Note: He is in favour of birth control, not against legal abortion, and not a Catholic. It should be entirely unnecessary - indeed, it should be inappropriate - to make such remarks together with a scientific or journalistic publication. Unfortunately, however, many people associate the opposite views with the idea that population growth is not economically detrimental, and that more people mean greater wealth rather than greater poverty in the long run. And they dismiss those ideas on the grounds of their supposed intellectual associations. That's why Peron feels - and rightly so - that he must tell you of his personal beliefs here.

It is the scientific data, not his ideology, that underlie Peron's conclusions. He provides an excellent overview of those data in this monograph, together with the theory that explains them. *Exploding Population Myths* is a fine introduction to the subject for those who have imbibed the conventional Malthusian ideas with their mothers' milk, and had the ideas reinforced by everyone from their teachers in elementary school to the newspapers and television in their adulthood. (Incidentally, Malthus himself rejected

"Malthusian" ideas in the second and subsequent editions of his book, after he gathered a body of facts and saw that this first-edition theory did not square with the facts, but you don't learn that in school or in the popular media.)

The current gloom-and-doom about a "crisis" of our environment is all wrong on the scientific facts. Even the official environmental protection agencies acknowledge that the air and water in the rich countries have been getting cleaner rather than dirtier in the past few decades. Every agricultrual economist knows that the world's population has been eating ever-better since World War II, defying simplistic Malthusian reasoning. Every resource economist knows that all natural resources have been getting more available rather than more scarce, as shown by their falling prices over the decades and centuries. And every demographer knows that the death rate has been falling all over the world - life expectancy almost tripling in the rich countries in the past two centuries, and almost doubling in the poor countries in just the past four decades. This is the most important and amazing demographic fact - the greatest human achievement in history. It took thousands of years to increase life expectancy at birth from just over 20 years to the high 20's in about 1750. Then life expectancy in the richest countries suddenly rose so that the length of life you could expect for your baby or yourself jumped from less than 30 years to perhaps 75 years. Then starting well after World War II, the length of life you could expect in the poor countries leapt upward by perhaps fifteen or even twenty years since the 1950s, caused by advances in agriculture, sanitation, and medicine. It is this decrease in the death rate that is the cause of there being a larger world population nowadays than in former times.

One would expect lovers of humanity to jump with joy at this triumph of human kind and organisation over the raw killing forces of nature. Instead, many lament that there are so many people alive to enjoy the gift of life, and even regret the decline in the death rate. And it is this worry that leads them to approve the Indonesian, Chinese and other inhumane programs of coercion and denial of personal liberty in one of the most precious choices a family can make - the number of children that it wishes to bear and raise.

The picture also is now clear that population growth does not hinder economic development. All the statistical studies show that faster population growth does not cause slower economic growth. In the 1980s there was a complete reversal in the consensus of thinking of population economists about the effects of more people. In 1986, the US National Research Council and the National Academy of Sciences completely overturned its "official" view away from the earlier worried view expressed in 1971. It noted the absence of any statistical evidence of a negative connection between population increase and economic growth. And it said that "The scarcity of exhaustible resources is at most a minor restraint on economic growth".

This U-turn by the scientific consensus of experts on the subject has gone unacknowledged by the press, the antinatalist environmental organisations, and the agencies that foster population control abroad.

Interestingly, though the classic sources from which Peron draws evidence are not new, absolutely nothing has changed in the long-run trends. It matters not for the main conclusions whether you were examining data in 1975 or now. We are not at a turning point in history.

For proper understanding of the important aspects of an economy we should look at the long-run trends. Almost every long-run trend in material human welfare points in a positive direction, as long as we view the matter over a reasonably long period of time. And there is no persuasive reason to believe that these trends will not continue indefinitely. But the short-run comparisons - between the sexes, age groups, races, political groups, which are usually purely relative - make more news.

The world's problem is not too many people, but lack of political and economic freedom. Blaming population for poor countries' problems is a tragic intellectual error. Read Jim Peron's book and you will have a sound basis for understanding these surprising phenomena.

Dr. Julian Simon is a professor at the University of Maryland business school and author of various books on the issue of population including *Population Matters, The Ultimate Resource,* and *The Economic Consequences of Immigration.*

A PERSONAL NOTE

The research and writing of this monograph has been a learning experience. I began my study with an open mind. While my previous readings have tended to indicate that the so-called overpopulation problem was exaggerated, I had not considered many of the facts I present here.

For reasons which I cannot understand, this is for many people, an emotional issue. It brings out the human passions and all the problems associated with non-rational thinking. The birth control movement, for example, has often launched unfair and bigoted attacks on opponents of population control. And because of these attacks it is my desire to lay my cards on the table.

I am not an opponent of birth control, nor would I make abortion illegal. I believe such issues should be decided by the individuals involved and not by the state. I do not believe that it is appropriate for any government to confiscate the wealth of its citizens in an attempt to promote one specific ideology - even if that ideology is my own.

It is often said that those who espouse the views I do are closet Catholics secretly pushing the Vatican line. But I am not a Catholic. I am an atheist.

I am not any of the things that the opposing camps on this issue use to stereotype each other. All things considered I am probably closer ideologically to those on the left when it comes to social issues in that I am anticensorship and prochoice.

But I feel that many "liberals" woefully lack an understanding of the economics involved. So while their sentiments are praiseworthy this lack of economic knowledge results in a misunderstanding of these issues. But this is not completely their fault as much of the material provided by the media and certain environmental groups is filled with myths and exaggerations.

It is to my friends in the population control movement that I present my arguments. As you read this monograph remember that I applaud much of your work. I admire your fight for the right of women to choose for themselves. I part company when the "right" to choose abortion becomes a mandate and when you use coercive methods of funding such as taxation. But I firmly believe that your intellectual honesty will cause you to question your own conclusions once the facts are presented. I do not question your motives but I assume that you have been spoon-fed myths and that your errors are the result of bad premises not bad intentions.

I would like to thank several people who contributed, either directly or indirectly to this manuscript. I want to thank Libby Husemeyer for her ruthless editing, which on some occasions I managed to fend off. I want to thank FMF Books for publishing the manuscript in South Africa; the Fraser Institute, my Canadian publisher; and the Heartland Institute, my American publisher. I should also thank Ludwig von Mises for making economics understandable. On a personal level I want to thank some dear friends who have encouraged and supported me: Frank Biafore III, Roger Miller and David Deysel.

 **THE MYTH OF FAMINE**

It is orthodox ideology today that overpopulation is a problem. We regularly hear dire warnings about the dangers it poses. But the term "overpopulation" is never defined. Exactly what is it? How do we know if a country is overpopulated? If overpopulation exists, is there such a thing as underpopulation?

For decades people have been announcing that China is "overpopulated", but no one has seemed overly concerned about the state of Maryland. Yet the population density (the number of people per square kilometre) in Maryland is much greater than in China. The United Kingdom also has a far higher population density than does China. Actually, the UK has a population density almost equal to that of "overpopulated" India. And Switzerland is more densely populated than Pakistan.

Clearly, some problems exist when it comes to defining our terms. If Maryland, the UK and Switzerland have greater population densities than India, China and Pakistan, then why are the latter considered overpopulated but not the former?

Defining the Problem

If we are to make any sense of the term "overpopulation", we need to be more careful in our use of the word. "Overpopulation" is meant to be a measure, but when we measure something we must have a point of reference. Presumably, if we know what "overpopulation" is, we should be able to state what the optimum population is as well, since the former term simply means "more than the correct population". Now, if this is our reference point, why has no one devised a formula for determining the correct population so that we know when we have exceeded that number?

The reason these terms are never defined is that to define the terms is to solve the problem... or, rather, to discover that there was no such problem in the first place. For instance, most people would probably agree that if people in a certain area die of starvation because food production cannot keep up with population growth, then the area is clearly overpopulated. The Environmental Fund certainly saw population growth and available food supply as co-factors in the "overpopulation" problem. In 1975 it ran a full-page ad in leading American newspapers announcing: "The world as we know it will likely be ruined before the year 2000 and the reason for this will be its inhabitants' failure to comprehend two facts. These facts are: 1. World food production cannot keep pace with the galloping growth of population. 2. 'Family Planning' cannot and will not, in the foreseeable future, check this runaway growth."[1] In other words, nothing could be done to prevent a major catastrophe because food production was declining on a per capita basis, and this catastrophe would strike "before the year 2000". We have almost reached the year 2000 and this prediction seems no closer to coming true today than it did in 1975. If anything, it now seems unlikely ever to come true!

Famine Everywhere

The Environmental Fund was not alone in its dire forecasts. Many others also saw a crisis looming. William and Paul Paddock, in their book *Famine - 1975!*, published in 1967, said that some nations were so far past salvation that a triage system must be instituted: Haiti, Egypt and India, for example, could never be saved and must be left to starve to death.2 Again, the mass starvation they predicted for these countries has not taken place and there is no reason to believe that it will any time in the near future.

Paul Ehrlich, the father of the overpopulation myth, has regularly predicted mass world starvation (among other catastrophes) ever since the early 1960s. Ehrlich confidently wrote in 1968 in *The Population Bomb* that there would be a major food shortage in the United States and that "in the 1970s...hundreds of millions of people are going to starve to death." He also claimed that by 1999 the US population would have declined to 22.6 million, less than 10% of its actual population as of 1994. He forecast that 65 million Americans would die of starvation between 1980 and 1989. He also thought that the oceans would be destroyed by 1979 and that fishing would collapse. For instance, he said that world fishing production in 1977 would be 30 million metric tons, whereas in reality it was 73 million metric tons, or well over twice what he predicted. Poor England fared even worse than the US in Ehrlich's scenario: "If I were a gambler, I would take even money that England will not exist in the year 2000."3

As far as Ehrlich was concerned, the "battle to feed all of humanity is over" and starvation has won. Luckily for us, reality has never caught up with Erhlich's scenarios.

Lester Brown of the Worldwatch Institute, another major environmental organisation, proclaimed in 1984 that "the period of global food security is over... the worldwide effort to expand food production is losing momentum... world food supplies are tightening and the slim margin between food production and population growth continues to narrow."4 Brown is a moderate, since he claimed only that the margin between food supplies and population was narrowing. In other words, unlike Ehrlich, he conceded that food production was increasing faster than population; he just believed it wouldn't continue. Ten years later that gap still hasn't closed. But Brown hasn't changed his tune: disaster is still just around the corner. His Worldwatch Institute released another report in January 1994 saying virtually the same thing as ten years earlier: "Seldom has the world faced an unfolding emergency whose dimensions are as clear as the growing imbalance between food and people."5 Media reports summarised the Institute's findings as follows: "The world appears near the limit of its ability to produce more food, and its exploding population must be controlled if people are to be adequately fed in coming decades."6

In his 1994 statement Brown emphasised that "[a]chieving a humane balance between food and people **now** depends more on family planners than on farmers" and "...we have enough data **now**. Unfortunately **now** I think we can see some of the constraints emerging more clearly"7 (my emphasis). Brown's statements make it sound as if it is only **now** that he has discerned this trend toward world famine; however, he has been beating that drum for years. And if, as he says, it is only **now** that the data have become available, then on what evidence did he base his claims from years ago? For instance, in 1967 he claimed, "The trend in grain stocks indicates clearly that 1961 marked a worldwide turning point... food consumption moved ahead of production."8 In 1984 he claimed that "we can see a clear breaking point somewhere around 1973."9

The US government contributed to the atmosphere of impending doom in the mid-1970s by sponsoring a travelling exhibit for schoolchildren titled, "Population: The Problem Is Us". The exhibit declared: "There are too many people in the world. We are running out of space. We are running out of energy. We are running out of food. And, although too few people seem to realize it, we are running out of time."[10] Children were told that "the birth rate must decrease and/or the death rate must increase." It reminded children that in times of famine "people have been known to eat dogs, cats, bird droppings, and even their own children." It showed a rat on a dinner plate and labeled it as future "food sources".[11] Books popular in "progressive" classrooms told schoolchildren that "world population is increasing at a rate of 2 percent per year whereas the food supply is increasing at a rate of 1 percent per year."[12] Even the United Nations joined the chorus. The UN Economic and Social Commission for Asia and the Pacific said in 1975 that there would be "500 million starvation deaths in Asia between 1980 and 2025". Yet Asia is now considered one of the major economic powerhouses of the world. The standard of living throughout Asia has been improving at phenomenal rates, and starvation and famine are virtually unheard of there.

We should note that dire warnings about population growth are nothing new and that modern doomsayers have many predecessors. Tertullian said, in 200 AD, "Most convincing as evidence of populousness, we men have actually become a burden to the earth, the fruits of nature hardly suffice to sustain us, there is a general pressure of scarcity giving rise to complaints, since the earth can no longer support us. Need we be astonished that plague and famine, warfare and earthquake come to be regarded as remedies, serving, as it were, to trim and prune the superfluity of population."[13] In the 4th century Saint Jerome made a similar observation: "The world is already full, and the population is too large for the soil."[14] At the time the world population was around 250,000,000, or approximately the population of today's United States. Like many doomsayers, Tertullian and Saint

Jerome simply assumed that they knew all there was to know. They were completely ignorant of the existence of North and South America, Australia, most of Africa, and parts of Asia and the South Pacific. In other words, they didn't know about the existence of most of the world!

The Abundance of Food

Measuring food production per capita actually isn't a bad way of determining overpopulation. The problem for the overpopulation panic-mongers is that if we use this definition, the "problem of overpopulation" has been decreasing each year even though the world has more and more people.

How can this be? Simply because there are two factors in the equation: the number of people, and the available food supply. If the world population is growing each year but the food supply is growing at a faster rate, then each year there will be more and more food per person. Under these circumstances we would have to say that each year the world is less overpopulated despite the increasing number of people. And the fact is that world food production *has* regularly and consistently grown at a faster rate than world population. That is the reason we don't worry about overpopulation in Maryland or England: though they have high population densities, both can feed their people without much difficulty.

Before looking at world population trends we should look at world food production. If we take caloric consumption as an indicator of how well fed the nations of the world are, we see some dramatic changes. In 1964-66 only 59 countries (that is, 42 percent of the world's total) recorded an average daily caloric consumption of at least 100 percent of requirements. Ten years later, in 1974-76, this was true of 72 countries (52 percent) and by 1982-84 this had increased again to 92

6

countries, or 66%.[15] Economist Jacqueline Kasun notes that

> ...world food production has increased considerably faster than population in recent decades. The increase in per capita food output between 1950 and 1977 amounted to either 28 percent or 37 percent, depending on whether United Nations or United States Department of Agriculture figures are used... More recent United Nations or United States Department of Agriculture data show that world food output has continued to match or outstrip population growth in the years since 1977. Some of the most dramatic increases have occurred in the poorest countries, those designated for "triage" by the apostles of doom. For example, rice and wheat production in India in 1983 was almost three-and-a-half times as great as in 1950. This was considerably more than twice the percentage increase in the population of India for the same period.[16]

Worldwide grain yields expanded by 2.6-fold between 1950 and 1984 "raising the grain consumed per capita by 40 percent."[17]

Nations where famine was common just a few years ago have now become food exporters. Only a few decades ago, for example, India was considered overpopulated and doomed to mass starvation; Paul Ehrlich wrote in 1968, "I have yet to meet anyone familiar with the situation who thinks India will be self-sufficient in food by 1971, if ever."[18] Yet India today exports food, and mass starvation is not very likely there any more. Ehrlich must have noted this himself, since in 1971 he quietly deleted this comment from his book

In 1981 Julian Simon, the bane of the overpopulation advocates, pointed out in the *Atlantic Monthly* :

> Net food grain availability—the amount available for human consumption—in kilograms per capita per year has been rising in India since at least 1950-51. Throughout the 1970s, food production increased at a faster rate than population. Why has India's food supply improved so dramatically? The cause is not an agronomic miracle but an expectable economic event. Most price controls on food were lifted, and price supports were substituted for controls. Indian farmers had a greater incentive to produce more, so they did. They increased production by planting more crops a year, on more land, and

by improving the land they had. They also introduced higher-yield strains and improved fertilizers.[19]

David Osterfeld writes:

> Since market-oriented reforms were introduced during the post-Mao period in China, food output has increased 40 percent, and China has now become a food exporter. Bangladesh, whose desperate plight inspired the first music relief concert in 1971, is now self-sufficient in food grains. And India, until just recently regarded as a hopeless basket case, has doubled its wheat production in less than 20 years, increased its rice output by 30 percent and its per capita food grain production by 7 percent, and is now a net food exporter. Indonesia, traditionally one of the world's largest importers of rice, is now rice self-sufficient. It has also made impressive gains in the production of cassava, sugar, and other products.[20]

In most of the world, food production is easily outstripping population growth, and on a worldwide basis the problem of overpopulation no longer exists. It is true, of course, that some nations still cannot feed themselves, but the reasons for this tend to be political. For instance, Cuba, once a highly industrialized and well-fed nation, is having major problems under Castro's brand of socialism. Zimbabwe has seen a massive decline in food production since independence, as have most of the emerging nations of Africa. But Africa is the last bastion of state planning and socialism, and it is no accident that it is also the last bastion of famine.

The dramatic rise in food production in Asia is testimony to the powerful effect that market-oriented reforms can have on an economy. Nations that abandon state economic planning for free markets see a dramatic increase in food production and even the poorest of the poor are better fed because of that increase. The crumbs of capitalism are capable of feeding more people than the planned banquets of socialism. This has been proved over and over again all around the world. As

Jacqueline Kasun says, "War and socialism are two great destroyers of the food supply in Africa, as they have been in other countries."[21]

The fact is that the world is easily capable of sustaining populations far in excess of current population figures even without developing any new farming methods or technologies. Roger Revelle, former director of the Harvard Center for Population Studies, estimated that the world could easily provide an adequate diet for 40 billion people. And his estimate assumed that the average yield per acre would be about one half what is currently produced in the United States. More surprisingly, he also argued that less-developed countries are capable of feeding 18 billion people and that Africa alone could produce enough food for 10 billion people.[22] In other words, Africa could feed the world twice over if its people were free to farm without state interference and socialist planning.

The former director of the Agricultural Economic Institute at Oxford University, Colin Clark, has estimated that if the world's farmers were to use the best methods of farming available, an American diet could be provided for 35.1 billion people. If a Japanese-style diet were provided, this number would be trebled.[23] The United Nations Population Fund has in essence acknowledged that famine is not very likely in the near future. A report by the UNPF

> ...dismisses fears of an overall global shortage of food of the kind much voiced by the Club of Rome school of forecasters some 20 years ago, pointing out that during the past 10 years, the world's food production has increased by 24%, outpacing the rate of population growth.
> ...The report concludes that.. production should be sufficient to meet all needs for the foreseeable future...[24]

THE MYTH OF SCARCE RESOURCES

What Is Scarcity?

We live in a world of scarcity. This is not a recent discovery of the environmental movement: economists have been studying the problem of scarce resources for centuries. In fact, without scarcity the field of economics would not exist, since economics is simply the study of the allocation of scarce natural resources to meet the needs and wants of humanity. If all goods were available in unlimited supplies, there would be no need to allocate them and thus no need for economics. Economist Thomas Sowell explains it this way:

> An economic system is a system for the production and distribution of goods and services. But what is crucial for understanding the way it functions is that it is a system for *rationing* goods and services that are *inadequate* to supply all that people want. This is true of any economic system, whether it is called capitalism, socialism, feudalism or by any other name. The Garden of Eden was not an economic system, even though it produced and distributed goods and services, because it produced them in such abundance that rationing was unnecessary. A utopia would not be an economic system for the same reason....
>
> Looked at another way, there are *inherent* constraints, given the limitations of nature and the unlimited desires of man, and economic systems are simply artificial schemes for administering the inherent scarcities. The scarcities themselves exist independently of the particular economic systems, and would exist if there were no economic system at all and people simply fought over everything they wanted. Economic institutions exist to introduce elements of rationality or efficiency into the use of inputs and outputs.
>
> The classic definition of economics is that it is the study of the allocation of scarce resources which have alternative uses. If resources—the ingredients of production—were not scarce, there would be no economics.[25]

Because all goods are scarce, they must be allocated, and that is what the price mechanism does. Prices restrict the demand for goods so that the quantity demanded is more in line with the quantity available or supplied. The greater the demand relative to supply, the higher the price, and the lower the demand relative to supply, the lower the price. But the very fact that a good or service has a price indicates that it is scarce. No scarcity - no price.

Abundance and Scarcity Together

Why am I emphasizing the scarcity of all goods when I have just been arguing that food supplies are abundant? For the very important reason that the term abundant does not mean unlimited. All natural resources are limited. Even in a world of abundance there are still limitations on what we can or cannot do. For example:

> Seawater has been estimated to contain 1 000 million years' supply of sodium chloride, magnesium and bromine; 100 million years' of sulphur, borax and potassium chloride; more than 1 million of molybdenum, uranium, tin and cobalt; more than 1 000 of nickel and copper. A cubic mile of seawater contains around 47 tons each of aluminium, iron, and zinc; given around 330-350 million cubic miles of such water, we are talking around 16 000 million tons each. Such estimates tend to exclude special concentrations such as the Red Sea brines and sediments; these alone contain perhaps $2 000 million worth of zinc, copper, silver and gold, and perhaps ten times this level, at current market prices.[26]

Now that sounds like a rather abundant supply, and it is. But we must remember that knowledge of a resource's existence is not the same thing as possessing it. Knowledge of the resource is just the first step. Next we must discover how to recover these resources, and then we must actually work to accomplish this goal. Finally, we must transport the resources to the locations where they are needed. Each of these steps requires the use of other resources – e.g. scientific knowledge, the ability to innovate, skilled labour, sophisticated equipment, ships, etc. – which are scarce and therefore costly. That is why the fact that minerals are abundant does not prevent them from simultaneously being scarce. Throughout this discussion it should be assumed that the word abundant does not imply the lack of scarcity. There is nothing that human beings want or need that isn't scarce.

Abundant is used here as a relative term, to indicate that some scarce goods are more abundant than others, or that some scarce goods are now more abundant than they once were. So we can argue that food supplies are becoming more abundant or less scarce. We can also argue that minerals and other resources are now less scarce than they once were. What we are discussing is relative scarcity.

But if we are measuring scarcity, we must have a yardstick to measure it by. In other words, we need to answer the question: how do we determine relative scarcity? Julian Simon puts it this way: "Ask yourself: If copper - or oil or any other good - were much scarcer today than it actually is, what would be the evidence of this scarcity? That is, what are the signs - the criteria - of a raw material being in short supply?"[27]

Simon notes that it isn't very likely that we will simply wake up one day to discover that a certain good has completely vanished. Long before a resource is depleted its supply begins to dwindle and individuals find it more difficult to obtain. The increased difficulty in obtaining the good will increase its price. And, of course, as the price goes up the demand goes down, thereby helping to conserve the good that has become scarcer. The best indicator of increasing or decreasing scarcity is price.

Now, we can measure price in several ways. We can either take the price of a good in terms of dollars, rands, pounds, yen, etc, or we can use the amount of labour necessary to obtain the good. Both methods have merits. Most people think in terms of monetary units like dollars, and there is nothing wrong with that as long as they remember that the monetary price of a resource may increase, not because the supply of the resource is becoming more scarce, but because the value of the money has been eroded by irresponsible government monetary policies. This is why economists adjust their calculations to take inflation into account.

There are also other circumstances in which temporary price distortions may give false signals about scarcity. For instance, during the 1970s the United States regulated the price of petrol, limiting what prices could be charged. As petrol became scarcer the price was not allowed to reflect the increased scarcity. As a result, consumers continued to demand an unrealistically high quantity of petrol and there was a fuel shortage, which created long lines at the pumps. The scarcer petrol was still being allocated, but not by the price - now it was allocated according to who could afford to wait in line. When the government deregulated the price of petrol, the queues disappeared and petrol eventually became even cheaper than it had been under the regulations.

The reverse may also occur. For instance, the South African government sets the price of petrol above its market rate, giving the impression that it is scarcer than it is. Various taxes, tariffs, environmental regulations and so on can also increase the price of a good above its market price. When this happens, consumer demand drops and producers find themselves with surpluses. Thus government interventions distort prices and this, in turn, distorts the economic decisions of consumers and producers. Prices are a means of transmitting information. High prices tell consumers to buy less and producers to produce more. Lower prices do the reverse. When governments tamper with prices they give consumers and producers the wrong message and waste scarce resources.

Sowell explains:

> How accurately... prices convey knowledge depends on how freely
> they fluctuate. The use of force to limit those fluctuations or to change
> the relationship of one price to another means that knowledge is
> distorted to represent not the terms of cooperation between A and B,
> but the force exerted by C. Looked at another way, the array of options
> people are willing to offer each other are reduced when force is applied
> to limit the level or the fluctuation of prices, and the array can shrink
> all the way to the vanishing point when the price is specified by the
> third party, if his specification does not happen to coincide with trade-
> offs mutually acceptable to entities contemplating transactions. Price
> fixing as a process cannot be defined by its hoped for results—"a
> decent wage", "reasonable farm prices", "affordable housing". Price
> fixing does not represent simply windfall gains and losses to particular
> groups according to whether the price happens to be set higher or
> lower than it would be otherwise. It represents a loss to the economy
> as a whole to the extent that many transactions *do not take place at all,*
> because the mutually acceptable possibilities have been reduced. The
> set of options simultaneously acceptable to A and B is almost
> inevitably greater than the set of options simultaneously acceptable to
> A, B, and C—where C is the third party observer with force, typically
> the government.[28]

It can also happen that the known supply of a resource diminishes
while the good simultaneously becomes less scarce. For instance, we
clearly have used a certain percentage of the world's copper, yet the
scarcity of copper has diminished. Why? The simple explanation is
that the demand for copper is falling relative to the supply of copper
available. Once we needed tons of copper for telephone cables: now
we use satellites, weighing only a tiny percentage of the cables, and
fiber optics for telecommunications.

Scarcity is affected by several factors:

- The known supply of any resource can increase dramatically with discoveries of previously unknown deposits.
- The supply can increase as new technologies allow resources to be tapped which previously were too expensive to use. For instance, iron ore supplies increase as new technologies allow us to mine lower grades of ore. In the 19th century only copper ores containing 4% to 6% copper were regarded as usable. Now copper ore with levels as low as 0.4% can be used.[29]
- New technologies or changing conditions may reduce the demand for a resource. The resource may be replaced by another, more abundant resource, or the amount needed to perform the same function may be reduced (as fiber optics has replaced copper telephone wires).
- New knowledge may create resources where previously none existed. For instance, oil was once considered a nuisance because we didn't know how to refine it for human use. Instead, whale oil was used. When the refining process was discovered the demand for whale oil plummeted while vast new resources, in the form of oil deposits, were created. Herman Kahn gives another example of this: "Until recently (1977), for example, the mineral nepheline (about 20 percent aluminum) was considered to be of little or no value. Now a technique has been developed for extracting its aluminum content, and it has been reclassified as a valuable raw material."[30]
- In unregulated markets, as a resource becomes more scarce its price increases, encouraging innovation. Consumers find ways of using less while producers find ways of producing more or of doing the same thing with other resources. The magic of the market is that these incentives are in direct proportion to the scarcity of the resources. The greater the scarcity, the greater the incentives.

Throughout human history these factors have appeared over and over again. The possible discoveries are endless, and each new discovery increases the options available to us. The microchip, for example, expanded possibilities – it didn't reduce them.

Now that we understand what economists mean by scarcity, it is possible for us to discover the answer to our fundamental question: is population growing while the resources needed to sustain human life are becoming more scarce?

Are We Running Out of Resources?

Since food production continues to outstrip population growth, we cannot say the world is overpopulated in relation to food. But perhaps other resources are becoming scarcer as time goes by. After all, we can grow food but we can't grow coal, oil or iron ore. And certainly the doomsayers of environmentalism have repeatedly warned us of the growing scarcity of natural resources. Fortunately, they have been just as wrong about this as they have been about food production.

The Limits to Growth, a popular doomsday book published in 1972, was considered to be a major work outlining the problem of resource depletion. Extrapolating from current trends, the authors attempted to show that the world was in dire danger of running out of virtually everything, and soon. The world would run out of gold by 1981, mercury and silver by 1985, tin by 1987, zinc by 1990, petroleum by 1992, and copper, lead and natural gas by 1993.[31] Similarly, Gordon Rattray Taylor, in his appropriately named *The Doomsday Book,* extrapolated from the fact that North Americans were using 50% of the world's resources in 1970 to conclude that "by 2000 they will, if permitted, be using *all* of them."[32] Well, extrapolating from past trends can be dangerous, especially if you ignore all the factors. Clearly the inhabitants of North America, in 1994, are not even close to using all the world's resources. Considering how rapidly Asia and South America are developing, along with the fact that there is no major decline in Europe or Australia, it is safe to say that North

America will not be able to grab all the world's resources in the next six years either! (For the record, Taylor also announced that "supplies of uranium at current prices... are expected to run out in the mid-1970s.")[33]

The world has been expecting to run out of oil ever since oil was first put to use. In 1885 the US Geological Survey announced that there was "little or no chance" of oil being discovered in California. A few years later, in 1891, it said the same thing about Kansas and Texas![34] The US Department of the Interior said in 1939 that American oil supplies would last only another 13 years. In 1949 the Secretary of the Interior announced that the end of the US supply of oil was in sight.[35] In 1974, learning nothing from past mistakes, the US Geological Survey announced that "at 1974 technology and 1974 price" the United States had only a 10-year supply of natural gas. The American Gas Association, on the other hand, disputed this and said that natural gas supplies were sufficient for the next 1,000 to 2,500 years.[36]

In 1952 the US President's Materials Policy Commission concluded that by the mid-1970s copper production in the States could not exceed 800,000 tons and that lead production would be at most 300,000 tons per year. But copper production in 1973 was 1.6 million tons and by 1974 lead production had reached 614,000 tons, i.e. 100% higher than predicted.[37]

Professor William Page of the Science Policy Research Unit at the University of Sussex notes that surveys of available minerals are continually discovering new supplies:

> In 1908, President Roosevelt called a meeting of State Governors in Washington, to discuss what to do about the apparent run-down of many mineral reserves. A large-scale survey of the USA was launched as a result and sufficient new deposits were found to alleviate concern. There have been a number of similar surveys conducted since then.

Had a 1944 review been correct, the Americans would by now have
totally exhausted their reserves of about 21 of the 41 commodities
examined. Tin, nickel, zinc, lead and manganese were on this short
list. But more has been found; more deposits (in terms of tons) were
found in the USA during the 1950s than during the previous 25 years.
Or take aluminium: between 1941 and 1953, known world bauxite
reserves grew by 50 million tons a year on average, while between
1950 and 1958 the average annual increase was about 250 million
tons.[38]

The economist Stanley Jevons predicted in 1865 that England
would soon run out of coal and that this would bring England's
factories to a standstill. Yet, as this is being written, the government
of John Major is embroiled in controversy because it is closing a
number of English coal mines. British coal is so plentiful, 130 years
after Jevon's prediction, that the government can't sell the mountains
of coal that have accumulated. Their only recourse is to shut down the
mines.

It has become so clear that mineral resources aren't being depleted
that even some environmental groups have conceded the fact. The
World Resource Institute estimates that the average price of all metals
and minerals actually fell 40% between 1970 and 1988.[39] And as any
economist can tell you, the best indicator of scarcity is price. The
amount of labour it takes to purchase the vast majority of goods and
services today is less than it was 20, 50 or 100 years ago. In other
words, virtually everything we need for our existence is becoming less
and less scarce each year!

Even the leading doomster, Paul Ehrlich, was forced to concede
that his predictions were in error when he accepted a bet with Julian
Simon. Ehrlich has continually attacked Simon and demeaned him as
a serious scholar, referring to his views as "examples of the sort of
blunders... economists of his ilk commit when they attempt to deal

with problems of pollution, resources and environment."[40]

In the midst of a heated exchange of papers between the two Simon flung down the gauntlet. He wrote:

> I'll put my money where my mouth is. This is a public offer to stake $10,000, in separate transactions of $1,000 or $100 each, on my belief that the cost of non-government-controlled raw materials (including grain and oil) will not rise in the long run. If you will pay me the current market price of $1000 or $100 worth of any standard mineral or other extractive product you name, and specify any date more than a year away, I will contract to pay you the then-current market price of the material. How about it, doomsayers and catastrophists? First come, first served.[41]

Ehrlich promptly responded that he would "accept Simon's astonishing offer before other greedy people jump in".[42] When the contract was drawn up, it differed from Simon's original version only in a few details.

Ronald Bailey reports:

> In October 1980, Ehrlich and Simon drew up a futures contract obligating Simon to sell Ehrlich the same quantities which could be purchased for $1,000 of five metals (copper, chrome, nickel, tin, and tungsten) ten years later at 1980 prices. If the combined prices rose above $1,000, Simon would pay the difference. If they fell below $1,000, Ehrlich would pay Simon. Ehrlich mailed Simon a check for $576.07 in October 1990. Simply put, the combined real prices of the metals selected by Ehrlich fell by more than 50 percent during the 1980s, confirming cornucopian claims that the supply of resources is becoming more abundant, not more scarce.[43]

Simon offered to renew the wager, but this time Ehrlich denounced the wager as a gimmick and refused to take part.

Why the Estimates Are Usually Wrong

Not only are the estimates of the reserves of various resources usually wrong, they are often wrong by huge percentages. The following chart, compiled by Herman Kahn, shows how the known reserve estimates of various ores have changed over the years.

KNOWN RESERVES IN METRIC TONS

ORE	1950	1970	%Increase
Iron	19,000,000	251,000,000	1,321
Manganese	500,000	635,000	27
Chromite	100,000	775,000	675
Tungsten	1,903	1,328	-30
Copper	100,000	279,000	179
Lead	40,000	86,000	115
Zinc	70,000	113,000	61
Tin	6,000	6,600	10
Bauxite	1,400,000	5,300,000	279
Potash	5,000,000	118,000,000	2,360
Phosphates	26,000,000	1,178,000,000	4,430
Oil	75,000,000	455,000,000	507

Figures like these are dramatic testimony to the underestimations that are continually made about the natural resources available for our use. In some cases, environmentalists deliberately underestimate resources in order to promote their own public policy agendas. Kahn gives an interesting example of this when he discusses aluminium reserves as stated in *The Limits to Growth*. According to *Limits* the world had only 33 to 49 years of aluminium resources left –and remember, it was written in 1974, which means that the world should be running out sometime between 2007 and 2023.

Kahn writes:

> Except for silicon (a semimetal), aluminum is the most abundant metal in the earth's crust, which contains about 8 percent aluminum, or roughly 2 million trillion tons. Can that much metal (or even .0001 percent of it) be used up in 49 years, the high side of Meadows' estimate? The resolution of the apparent confusion lies in Meadows' footnotes, where he explains that he has counted only the aluminum in *known reserves of bauxite.* In other words, if we ignore every possible source of aluminum except known high-grade bauxite deposits, we will come up with this number. Or will we? No, not even then. For even though he states in a footnote that unless otherwise specified he will use data from the 1973 U.S. Geological Survey document *U.S. Mineral Resources,* in the case of aluminum there is another footnote explaining that he has taken the estimate from the earlier U.S. Bureau of Mines report *Mineral Facts and Problems, 1970,* which happened to use a 1965 estimate that was less than half the one given in the 1973 document. Moreover, the later volume unambiguously asserts in a summary statement that "... the nation has virtually inexhaustible potential resources of aluminous materials other than bauxite," and it proceeds to describe 10 of them.... [a single of which] contains more aluminum than Meadows' estimate for total known world reserves plus potential future reserves.[44]

Kahn points out similar distortions regarding other metals such as iron. Meadows contended that the world iron supply would not last beyond the year 2128. Yet iron, like aluminium, is one of the most plentiful metals in the earth's crust.

Nobody Is Looking

Huge discrepancies like these may give rise to charges of dishonesty. But – a few deliberate distortions aside – there are good reasons why these estimates continue to be off by such large percentages. The fact is that we have no need for accurate estimates since we are not in danger of running out of any of the major natural resources that we need. *Report on the Limits to Growth* by the World Bank explained it this way:

> We do not know the true extent of the resources that exist in, and can ultimately be recovered from, the earth. Nor will we know in the next two years or ten years. The reason why we do not know the absolute limits of the resources we have is simple and does not even require recourse to elaborate arguments about the wonders of technology. We do not know because no one has as yet found it necessary to know and therefore went about taking an accurate inventory.[45]

Most of us are familiar with this phenomenon on a day-to-day level. Have you ever decided to go shopping only to find you don't have enough money for whatever it is that you need? You start checking your jacket pockets and look in drawers and under the cushions of the sofa. And often you find enough spare change and forgotten notes to cover the cost of the desired item. These financial resources were there the day before but you didn't look for them because you didn't need them.

Neither the businesses that depend on these resources nor the mining companies that mine them are interested in investing large sums of money to locate resources which they have no need for in the foreseeable future. The estimates, however, continue to grow because we continue to stumble, without much effort, on new reserves. In a few cases temporary panics produce large reserves by acting as a spur to systematic exploration – there was a dramatic increase in oil reserves as a result of the oil crisis of the 1970s, for example. Wilfred Beckerman of the University of London explains it like this:

> At no point is it worth prospecting for enough to last to the end of eternity, or even some compromise period, such as a hundred million years, or even 1,000 years. New reserves are found, on the whole, as they are needed, and needs do not always rise exponentially at past rates. In fact, given the natural concentrations of the key metals in the earth's crust, as indicated by a large number of random samples, the total natural occurrence of most metals in the

top mile of the earth's crust has been estimated to be about a million times as great as present known reserves. Since the latter amount to about 100 years' supplies this means we have enough to last about one hundred million years.[46]

Furthermore, it is a mistake to think only about underground resources: there are millions of tons of metals and minerals that, at the right price, can be recycled from above-ground sources. This lesson was learned by the Hunt brothers when they attempted to corner the world silver market in the 1970s. Using their vast resources they began to buy up all the silver they could find. As a result silver prices went through the ceiling, soaring from just a few dollars an ounce to over $50.

But then several things happened. Out of the woodwork came a flood of silver. People searched their attics for stray silverware, candlesticks, rings, etc. Some people had silver fillings removed from their teeth and replaced with less valuable substitutes. Old silver coins, previously worth little, were suddenly relatively valuable and joined the flood. Meanwhile, silver mines found they could afford to mine less valuable ore since the price of silver was so high. Soon the market was awash with a veritable flood of silver. Silver prices plummeted and the Hunts lost a bundle. Their attempt to corner the silver market resulted only in the redistribution of their wealth to thousands of others, who suddenly found themselves with windfall profits.

We can assume that the same set of economic incentives will be created by a *natural* shortage of any resource as well. The higher price will encourage recycling, cheaper substitutes will drive down demand, and new stockpiles will be located. The Hunt brothers learned a lesson about economic incentives and the scarcity of resources. Now if only the environmentalists would learn the same lesson.

One fundamental error that is made not just by environmentalists but by politicians and many others is to take a current trend and project it into the future. Almost without exception such projections are virtually worthless because they ignore the fact that changing conditions change incentives, which in turn change human behaviour. Max Singer referred to this desire to project into the future as the Gary Cooper effect, based on an old film he saw. Singer said the film was

> a piece of froth in which the humor was based on Cooper, playing Hollywood's idea of a typical masculine engineer in those days, having to take care of a baby without any woman to help him. He was doing fine applying his engineering training and masculine logic to the tasks of diapering, feeding, burping, etc. But one thing troubled him. He reported to his friend that the baby's weight had already increased by 20% and that at that rate it would weigh over a hundred pounds before it was a year old, and he didn't know what to do about it.[47]

Projections based on current trends usually assume that humans are incapable of change – that they are mindless creatures who will continue behaving as they have always behaved despite changes in circumstances. Paul Ehrlich uses examples of animal behaviour and then tries to extrapolate to humans. He argues: "To ecologists who study animals, food and population often seem like sides of the same coin. If too many animals are devouring it, the food supply declines; too little food, the supply of animals declines... Homo sapiens is no exception to that rule, and at the moment it seems likely that food will be our limiting resource."[48] Yet we know this is not true. We know that rising prices encourage lower consumption and increased production. We know that when an economy prospers the birth rate declines, often to the point where there is negative population growth. We know that humans **do** respond to incentives and change their behaviour. And this is a major reason the doomsday predictions have been wrong: they forget that people have minds. As Nick Eberstadt of the Harvard Population Center pointed out, "One of the reasons that Ehrlich's been so wrong is that he has no understanding of, or sympathy for, the economic process that human beings engage in."[49]

THE MYTH OF OVERCROWDING

Are We Really Overcrowded?

Food production continues to exceed population growth, and non-renewable resources seem to become more plentiful each year. Thus we can't use either of these two factors to prove overpopulation. So . we must turn instead to other factors.

The weakest basis for defining overpopulation is that of population density. Instead of arguing that we are running out of food or resources, this argument says we are running out of space. And the doomsayers, predictably, have painted graphic pictures of the disasters that await humanity because of overcrowding. In *The Doomsday Book* Gordon Rattray Taylor discusses a small herd of deer released on James Island in Chesapeake Bay. The herd built up for a number of years, but then mysteriously, almost two thirds of them died off around 1958. His conclusion is that the deer died from stress. While acknowledging that the winter of 1958 was particularly cold, Taylor says this "would not in itself account for such a massive die-off."[50] Taylor believes that the stress was caused, not by a lack of food or other resources, but by crowding – though not extreme crowding.

Taylor then proclaims that "[m]an is in no way exempted from the laws of population growth."[51] He writes that if all humans were to spread themselves as far away from each other as possible, "each man, woman, or child would find him or herself about 150 yards from his nearest neighbor. By the year 2000, the distance will have shrunk to 120 yards and by 2070 to 60 yards. Imagine the plains of the Middle

West with dwellings 120 yards apart in every direction and you have the picture. When the deer on James Island began to die of brain haemorrhages they were about 80 yards apart."[52] The implications are clear: a great human die-off is awaiting us when we become overcrowded as a result of overpopulation. But, if this is so, why hasn't the die-off already begun in places like Hong Kong, London, Mexico City and Tokyo?

Certainly Taylor's theory doesn't require that all human beings on the planet be overcrowded before the die-off materialises. After all, it was only the deer on James Island that were crowded, not all the deer in the world. The fact is, the theory that stress caused the death of the James Island deer has yet to be proved. It is simply a hypothesis. And even if it were proved, Taylor shows no correlation between deer and humans. While many mammals are solitary or live in relatively small groups, humans, throughout evolution, have been social creatures. And ever since technology and medicine have allowed it, human groupings have been extremely large with millions of people living, by choice, within a relatively small area. Perhaps humans, unlike deer, *require* a certain amount of crowding. Jonathan Freedman, a former associate of Ehrlich, writes, in his book *Crowding and Behavior:* "People who live under crowded conditions do not suffer from being crowded. Other things being equal, they are no worse off than other people."[53]

And just how overcrowded are we anyway? Certainly the world is filled with empty places. A flight almost anywhere in the world reveals vast expanses of unoccupied land. Cities cover only a very small percentage of the earth. When we look at the world's population relative to land available, we find out just how "underpopulated" the world is:

> Just how many people are there on the earth? To say there are around five billion means very little to most people. Instead, that number can be put in

Population density per square mile for some of the major cities of the world.

Hong Kong*	247,501
Bombay	127,461
Madrid	68,385
Bangkok	58,379
Lima	56,794
Manilla	54,024
Rome	43,949
Mexico City	40,037
Beijing	38,156
Singapore	34,856
Athens	30,237
Moscow	27,562
Tokyo/Yokohama	25,019
New York	11,480
Sydney	10,460
London	10,429
Los Angeles	9,126
Chicago	8,568
Miami	7,748
Houston	7,512

* This density is for Hong Kong city, the entire territory has a lower density of 13,288.

perspective by asking what would happen if the world's people were put into the land area of Texas: each person would have an area equal to the floor space of a typical U.S. home. Indeed, some cities in the United States, such as Jacksonville, Florida, contain enough land area to provide standing room for the entire global population.[54]

It has been argued that land per se is not an important issue. After all, who will farm in Antarctica or in the Sahara? The real question is that of arable land. But this overlooks the economic benefits of land for purposes other than farming. Certainly much of the land in Kuwait is useless for agricultural purposes, but it does contain petroleum. In a market economy land is allocated to its most useful purpose. If farm land became scarce enough to threaten our survival as a species, its price would increase dramatically and farm land that had been paved over with shopping malls would be converted back to farm land. Malls would be torn down and farms built in their stead. Thomas Sowell notes:

> Even if one were to use arable land as the standard, it would change no fundamental conclusions. Japan, for example, compares even more unfavorably to India on the basis of arable land than of land in general, but it is India that [had] famines. Similarly, famine-stricken Ethiopia has many times more acres of arable land per capita than Singapore or Great Britain. As a distinguished specialist in under-developed economies has pointed out, 'famines and food shortages occur mostly in sparsely populated subsistence economies with abundant land'.[55]

It has been alleged that the world is rapidly losing access to all farm land, but this simply isn't true. In fact, the amount of land suitable for agricultural purposes has been increasing. It is believed that the world currently uses only one-third of the agricultural land available. And if there *is* global warming, which is far from proven, higher temperatures will increase the total land available for agricultural purposes while increased CO_2 levels will help stimulate plant growth.[56]

Crowded By Choice

What many doomsayers forget is that the vast majority of people live in densely populated areas by choice. Indeed, the worldwide trend is for people to move from less populated areas to more populated areas. And the reasons for this are relatively sound. The larger the number of individuals, the greater the number of trade transactions that are possible. The greater the number of possible transactions, the wealthier the community. This is why urban areas tend to be wealthier than rural areas.

Moreover, certain technologies that improve the standard of living are prohibitively expensive in rural areas but relatively cheap in densely populated cities. This is one reason why you never see subway systems in farming communities: the economies of scale don't allow for them. The same is true for highways, hospitals, electricity, sewerage systems and other services. The rural areas have more than enough land for everyone and we could shut down the densely populated cities. But we don't. To do so would be folly and would make all of us poorer. Professor Nathan Keyfitz says that the concentration of capital in cities allows for healthier lifestyles, in spite of the problems usually associated with crowding: "...the concentration of people in cities has much to be said for it. To be sure the air above Mexico City is scarcely breathable – but this is a local effect. In spite of the bad air, city dwellers live longer than their country cousins. Certainly health care, education and other amenities are more easily provided to urban populations than to rural ones."[57]

Environmentalists should actually applaud cities and dense population concentrations since these are more environmentally friendly than spreading out. Individuals in densely populated regions don't need to use as many resources to travel to work: they often walk, or use buses or trains instead of cars. City dwellers use less land per person for living. Not only that, but the amount of natural resources used to build the typical city dwelling is considerably less than the amount used for rural or suburban dwellings. City dwellers tend to live in smaller homes than their rural counterparts. High population densities in the cities leave large tracts of land open for recreational, agricultural or conservation purposes. Keyfitz puts it this way: "When people are concentrated in cities, they would seem to have less direct effect on the forests, the wildlife, the oceans–on the biosphere in general."[58]

And, generally speaking, the denser the population, the wealthier the citizens. For instance, Hong Kong has a population density of 247,501 per square mile, Japan 850, Singapore 12,200, Taiwan 1,478 and South Korea 1,134. By contrast, India's population density is 683 per square mile, China's 409 and Pakistan's 378. As we pointed out earlier, many of the wealthier parts of the world have much higher population densities than so-called "overpopulated" poor areas. Jacqueline Kasun writes, "There is no evidence that more densely settled populations tend to have lower levels of per capita income and output... Some of the most densely settled countries in the world...have very high levels of per capita income and output."[59] She also notes:

> Within all countries, however, the most densely settled areas—the cities—have the highest levels of per capita output and income. Economists have long explained these relationships on the grounds mentioned above—the more densely settled populations make better use of their transportation and communications systems as well as other parts of their economic infrastructure. They also have more opportunities for face-to-face contacts that encourage innovation and productivity.
>
> Larger populations not only inspire more ideas but more *exchanges*, or improvements, of ideas among people, in a ratio that is necessarily more than proportional to the number of additional people. (For example, if one person joins an existing couple, the possible number of exchanges does not increase by one-third but triples.) One of the advantages of cities, as well as of large universities, is that they are mentally stimulating, that they foster creativity.[60]

The point about increased trade is important, since the greater the

Does Population Density Decrease Wealth?

The population density of Malaysia is 141 per square mile. Singapore with a population density of 34,856 per square mile is a whopping 247 times more crowded. Yet the per capita Gross National Product of Singapore is $12,200 while for Malaysia it is $2,460.

Compare the per capita Gross Domestic Product (in 1988) for the following:

	GDP per capita	Population density
China	$320	409
Taiwan	$4,325	1,478
Hong Kong	$8,260	247,501

number of choices, the greater the likelihood that an individual will find an exchange that will increase his personal well-being.

Ester Boserup, in *Population and Technological Change,* reflects on the historical relationship between population density and technological advancement. She concludes:

> ...before the industrial revolution one densely populated area after another became the technological leader. During the whole of this part of human history, the main advantage of a dense population, i.e., the better possibilities to create infrastructure, seems to have outbalanced the disadvantages of a less favourable ratio between population and natural resources. Europe succeeded Asia as the technological leader, but only after it arrived at relatively high population densities... [T]he inhabitants of large sparsely populated continents were doomed to be illiterate subsistence producers.[61]

Of course there are disadvantages to living in densely populated regions, but clearly the benefits must outweigh the costs. Economically speaking we can determine the values of people, not by their assertions, but by their actions. The fact that so many of us choose to live in cities is sufficient proof that we find them beneficial.

And Things Are Only Getting Better

We all know that the world's population is increasing each day. And for the forseeable future it will continue to increase, but a trend is clearly emerging. This trend seems to indicate that the world population will begin to level off and then fall.

Herman Kahn believes there are three stages of population growth. The first was the early period of man's existence when both birth rates and death rates were high. This led to a long period of population stability. Then, "as the process of economic and technological development gathered momentum, following the onset of industrialisation, productivity increased and food distribution was regularized – reducing famines and famine-induced disease –and more resources were devoted to improvements in public health and safety. The consequent decline in death rates – with birth rates remaining high –caused a rapidly increasing population."[62] Eventually a third stage was reached where "parents began to have fewer and fewer children, prompted by the reduced value of children as economic assets combined with the increased cost of rearing them and the erosion of traditional religious and social pressures for large families."[63] This, he believes, will continue until the birth rate slows sufficiently to bring about a static population, and eventually a decline. Thus while there is a massive blip on the chart showing the rapid increase of the world's population over the last two hundred years, Kahn believes that population will decline just as rapidly over the next two hundred years.

Certain demographic trends seem to support this theory, for in much of the world we have already reached the stage of stable or diminishing populations. Certainly the peak in population growth appears to have occurred around 1970 when the world's population was growing at a rate of 2.09% per year. By 1980 that growth rate was down to 1.73%, and by 1990 to 1.7%.[64] In the last five years the drop in population growth has been even more dramatic. According to the Institute for Demographic Studies the growth in world population has now declined to 1.5%.[65] Thus the populatin growth rate in the last five years has dropped much faster than in the previous decade. Thomas Merrick, president of the Population Reference Bureau, believes that within the next hundred years the world will reach the zero population growth rate. He says, "World population is on the path toward stabilisation."[66] Merrick, considered an optimist by some, may be wrong. At current rates world population stability will be reached within 30 years.

If we look at the Total Fertility Rate for the various regions of the world we see a massive decline everywhere except in Africa. The world rate during 1950-55 was five children per woman but for the period of 1980-85 this had declined to 3.6. With 2.1 being needed for zero population growth, the world has moved almost halfway toward this goal in just 30 years. Ben Wattenberg notes, "As recently as 1970, women in the less-developed world were bearing a lifetime average of 6.1 children. Today it is 4.1. "[67] In the decade since Wattenberg wrote the average fertility rate has dropped to 3.1.[68] The more developed countries have already achieved a TFR of 2.0, below the replacement level. East Asia has declined from 5.5 to 2.3, Asia, as a whole, has dropped from 6.0 to 3.9, and Central America has fallen from 6.8 to 4.8.[69]

People have grown used to referring to the impoverished nations of the world as the "Third World," but the Third World is now almost exclusively Africa. Poverty is diminishing at a rapid pace in Asia, and South and Central America are also experiencing general levels of increased prosperity. With few exceptions, almost all the nations reporting negative or stagnant growth are in Africa. And it is in Africa where the TFR has remained almost stagnant as well. But this is not unusual. Economists have long understood the relationship between economics and birth rates.

So not only is world food production growing faster than the world's population, but it is continuing to increase while world population rates are declining. Contrary to what people assume, the world isn't becoming more overpopulated. In fact, it is becoming less overpopulated every year. Unless there is a wholesale adoption of socialist economics, there is no reason to believe that this situation will change any time in the near future. Each day that goes by, there is more food per person than the day before. The "good old days" are still ahead of us. D. Gale Johnson, an agricultural expert with the University of Chicago, sums up the current state of affairs: "Except where civil wars exist or despotic governments prevail, there has never been a time during the last two centuries when the people in the developing world were better fed or when their food supply was more secure... The scourge of famine due to natural causes has been almost conquered and could be entirely eliminated by the end of the century."[70]

It Pays to Have Babies - Lots of Them

In poor countries children are often seen as a retirement plan. Parents need someone to provide for them in their old age and children are the means to this end. However, with relatively high death rates plaguing the society, the only way to ensure that your retirement plan will still exist when you grow old is to have as many children as possible. Osterfeld notes:

> High fertility rates were necessary to offset the high mortality rates. In both preindustrial societies of historical times and nonindustrial societies of today, nearly all the incentives are to have large families. First, the cost of rearing children is minimal and by the time they are 5 or 6 years old they are working in the fields or doing other odd jobs and more than 'paying their way.' The man with many children controls much wealth. In terms of economic production more children mean an increased supply of food and perhaps the production of surpluses for trade. In such societies children also provide the only support for parents in their old age... Many children, especially where mortality rates are high, provide an important hedge against the uncertainties of the future; it is a rational way both to minimize risks and to maximize the possibility of wealth. 'The very poor even in industrial societies,' wrote Benedict, 'can often see no advantage in limiting their children. At the lowest levels 10 children are no more of a handicap than 9. The child as yet unborn may be the very one who will help his parents.'[71]

An example of this logic comes from India, where a Punjabi water carrier told an anthropologist whom he mistook for a family planner that had visited him many years earlier: "You were trying to convince me...that I shouldn't have any more sons. Now, you see, I have six sons and two daughters and I sit at home in leisure. They are grown up and

37

they bring me money. One even works outside the village as a labourer. You told me I was a poor man and couldn't support a large family. Now you see, because of my large family, I am a rich man."[72]

In an industrialised economy, raising a child is expensive, and the higher the income of the family the greater the costs. If the woman works, she will have to forego her usual income during the later stages of pregnancy and often during the first few years of the child's life. At the same time, with retirement plans, pensions, and so on, few people in developed countries look to their children for support in their old age. But in poor, undeveloped countries the opposite is true. With minimal employment available, the woman doesn't sacrifice much to have a child and each child soon becomes a net benefactor to the parents. Kasun notes:

> In societies where children begin to work at a young age, where their mothers do not work, and where they do not receive long, expensive educations, big families cost relatively little. Large families even add to the welfare of the whole. Economies of scale, familiar enough in industry, apply equally to families... But in developed, urbanized, industrial society all this changes... The costs of children rise disproportionately to the increases in income that development brings; and the average family size falls. Unsurprisingly, in the industrialized countries population growth rates are now below replacement levels and population is declining in several of them[73]

Barbara Klugman, a social anthropologist at the Centre for Health Policy Studies at the University of the Witwatersrand, makes the same point:

> In an extended family situation, children usually contribute to the family income. Thus in the present situation of widespread unemployment, the more children one has, the greater the chance that at least some will gain employment.
>
> Both as a cultural pattern and because of the lack of adequate social security benefits, poor people rely on children to support and look after them in their old age...
>
> Having only one or two children is no guarantee that a rural African

person will see any children live into their adulthood, as a result of the higher infant mortality rate. And until such time as those factors which cause high infant mortality change, people will continue to have many children. To date no country has achieved a low birthrate as long as it has had a high infant mortality rate.[74]

What is clear is that as a country develops economically, birth rates decline. Thus if we want to reduce population growth we must promote economic growth, and that means that we must promote a free economy. State central economic planning doesn't work. More importantly, as Mises and Hayek have proved, it *cannot* work.[75] The only economic system that has successfully raised the standard of living of a vast number of people for an extended period of time is market capitalism. This isn't even a debatable point any more – even well-known socialist Robert Heilbroner has admitted: "Less than seventy-five years after it officially began, the contest between capitalism and socialism is over: capitalism has won. The Soviet Union, China, and Eastern Europe have given us the clearest possible proof that capitalism organizes the material affairs of humankind more satisfactorily than socialism: that however inequitably or irresponsibly the marketplace may distribute goods, it does so better than the queues of a planned economy."[76]

Economic development, more than family planning programmes, free birth control or anything else, will bring about a population decline in the less developed countries. Ironically, the pressure groups concerned about population growth are promoting policies that discourage growth. Bolch and Lyons note:

> Paradoxically, one way to cause the growth rate of population to slow in the long run (but not in the short) may be to follow economic policies that are associated with a reduction in the mortality rate: the creation of institutions that will allow sustained economic growth, something that is almost always accompanied by improvements in both private health care and public health facilities. Two principal reasons why population rates have slowed toward zero or even negative levels in much of the industrialized world are first, the

If Everyone in the World Moved...

...to the US state of Texas the population density per square mile would be 20,705.... or almost the same as Paris, France (20,185) or Toronto, Canada (20,420).

...to South Africa the population density would be 11,502.... that is less than Budapest (16,691) or Milan (13,806) and about the same as Berlin (11,026)

...to the United States the population density would be 1,531... this would be about the same as Mauritius, a popular resort site in the Indian Ocean.

relative security that higher levels of income and wealth provide, and second, the increased freedom for women that generally accompanies economic growth. By promoting ecologically driven policies that seek to limit economic growth, the environmental movement may be ensuring the defeat of one of its basic aspirations.[77]

4 POPULATION POLITICS

Ideas have consequences. And the idea that the world is overpopulated leads to certain inescapable conclusions. If there are too many people in the world, then each newborn is a threat to every other human being. If these babies are threats, then it would be acceptable to eradicate the threat. Now, this may sound harsh and unrealistic. After all, most population control groups don't actually advocate the eradication of children.

But many of these groups come very close to this view when they argue that unless people "voluntarily" restrict their family size it should be done "coercively". In his book *Population, Resources, Environment,* Ehrlich acknowledges that "compulsory control of family size is an unpalatable idea to many, but the alternatives may be much more horrifying."[78] On another occasion Ehrlich compares children to cancer: "We can no longer afford merely to treat the symptoms of the cancer of population growth; the cancer itself must be cut out."[79] Another advocate of population control, Kingsley Davis, says, "Over-reproduction – that is, the bearing of more than four children – is a worse crime than most and should be outlawed."[80] Biologist Paul Silverman told one university audience, "If voluntary restraints on population growth are not forthcoming we will be faced with a need to consider coercive measures."[81]

Myths affect public policy. An interesting example of this is Adolph Hitler's policy of *Lebensraum*. Hitler wanted to expand the territory under German control because he believed that Germany was becoming overpopulated and soon would not be able to feed its people. On January 21, 1938 Hitler told his generals:

> A good harvest provides just enough food for our present population for one year. If the harvest is only mediocre, we lose several months' food supplies. If the harvest is poor – and this will certainly happen one day – the German people will only get enough food for quarter or half a year-on the basis of the *present* population, that is. But Germany's population growth is 600,000 new heads every year. That's six million in ten years. How can Germany continue to feed her people? That is only possible if we acquire new territory - and we must get that by brute force.[82]

The flaw in Hitler's reasoning was that he assumed that agricultural output couldn't be increased more rapidly than population growth without territorial conquest. This same logic is behind the entire overpopulation hysteria. The proof of his error is that Germany today has a much larger population than it had in 1938 and yet it is one of the richest countries in the world. The two projections that Hitler made – that population would continue to grow and that agricultural output would be stagnant – were both wrong. Food production grew faster than did the population, and today the German birth rate is well below the replacement level.

Coercive Population Control

Ehrlich begins with the same premises as Hitler but he tackles the issue from the opposite direction; in other words, whereas Hitler's solution was to forcibly expand agricultural output, Ehrlich's solution is to forcibly limit population growth.

Coercive methods of birth control have been used in a number of Third World countries. Anthropologist Steven Mosher, who lived in rural China when the "one child" policy of the government was implemented, describes what happened there:

> ...there were eighteen women, all from five- to nine-months pregnant, and many red-eyed from lack of sleep and crying. They sat listlessly on short plank benches in a semicircle about the front of the room, where He Kaifeng [a top cadre and party member] explained the purpose of the meeting in no uncertain terms. "You are here because you have yet to 'think clear' about birth control, and you will remain here until you do." ...Looking coldly around the room, he said slowly and deliberately, "None of you has any choice in this matter...." Then, visually calculating how far along the women in the room were, he went on to add, "The two of you who are eight or nine months pregnant will have a Caesarean; the rest of you will have a shot which will cause you to abort."[83]

The New York Times reported in 1982 that Chinese women were "rounded up and forced to have abortions." The article by Christopher Wren said that "vigilantes abducted pregnant women on the streets and hauled them off, sometimes handcuffed or trussed, to abortion clinics."[84]

Mosher describes the pain of one woman whose pregnancy was discovered at the last minute. She pleaded to be allowed to have one more child. "In the village there is no way to survive if you don't have a son," she cried. In the rural areas of China as in many other parts of the underdeveloped world, children were regarded as a means of support for parents in their old age. Since a son was more likely than a daughter to be able to provide for his parents, many families wanted to have at least one son. But if they were allowed only one child and that child was a girl, they were faced with a problem. Many rural families solved this problem by simply allowing female babies to die. In an article for the *Wall Street Journal* Mosher wrote that the *People's Republic Press* openly spoke of the "butchering, drowning, and leaving to die of female infants and the maltreating of women who have given birth to girls."[85] A policy to "limit" population growth actually resulted in the genocide of female children.

In the Dongpu district of Canton birth control regulations that came into effect in 1987 stated that any unmarried pregnant woman "should be ordered to have an abortion". A woman was required to have an IUD inserted within four months of having her first child. Any woman "who has had one child [who] fails at birth control" would be forced to have an abortion and undergo sterilisation. According to *China Spring* the regulations further stated, "If any unauthorized baby dies within three months of birth, the penalty will be only 300 yuan." This penalty is less than a mother would have to pay for having an "unauthorised" child and it is therefore a blatant attempt to encourage infanticide.[86]

In another case the Chinese government tried to force a Chinese woman, studying with her husband in the United States, to have an abortion. The woman, who was pregnant with her second child, received a letter from the Population Control Office of the Manchurian factory where she had previously worked. The letter said:

> The punishment for this kind of violation is very severe, and we strongly advise you not to risk it.
> If you cannot have this abortion done abroad, then the factory director orders you to return to China immediately. Any further delays, and you will be punished according to the law.
> There is nothing ambiguous about our order! Make up your mind immediately.[87]

The US government, through the Agency for International Development, was involved in this "birth control" programme. AID "disclaimed direct involvement in the program, although it was a major contributor to the International Planned Parenthood Federation and the UN Fund for Population Activities (UNFPA), both of which supplied funds to the Chinese program."[88]

Forced abortion and the murder of babies in Communist China, like Hitler's *Lebensraum* policy, were direct results of accepting the overpopulation myth. Nick Eberstadt writes that the Chinese policy was implemented because the government "had decided that its modernization program was being threatened by 'excessive' childbearing in the provinces (the role of the government in depressing the production of food or restricting the expansion of consumer industries was not a subject for public discussion)."[89] The Chinese saw coercive birth control as just another form of socialism. According to a member of China's Family Planning Commission,

> ...social production is composed of material production and human reproduction...The socialist system in China [emphasizes both] material production and human reproduction, and [must] regulate population growth in a planned way, as we regulate material production following plans.[90]

The Chinese programme was not condemned by the population control movement. On the contrary, many groups applauded the use of raw coercion.. UNFPA gave an award to China for its attempts to control population growth. Another group, Californians for Population Stabilization, held an "Award Dinner in Honor of The People's Republic of China" to honor the Communist Chinese "for acknowledging overpopulation and encouraging family planning". The main speaker at the award dinner was the president of the Population Institute.

When a number of individuals within the American government became disturbed that taxpayers' money was being channeled through private groups to help finance coercive "population control" in China and attempted to stop these grants, Planned Parenthood, which receives millions in taxpayer funding, launched a vigorous lobbying effort to counter the proposal. The campaign scrupulously avoided all mention of the Chinese connection, implying instead that right-wing fanatics were trying to destroy birth control around the world. One ad, which ran in *The Washington Post*, was headed "The Right-Wing Coup in

Family Planning". It claimed:

> For two decades, poverty-stricken Third World countries have turned to the United States for help with their vital family planning efforts.
>
> The aid has only cost you about a dollar a year, but the impact has been tremendous. Rapid population growth has slowed in some countries. In others, even the poorest families have been given the means to plan their own futures.
>
> Millions of children have been spared the ravages of hunger. Thousands of women are alive today who would have died in their ninth or tenth or sixteenth pregnancy.
>
> Planned Parenthood is proud to have played a leading role in helping the people in more than fifty nations help themselves. Where there was only desperation, we have brought hope.
>
> Incredibly, however, everything we have achieved is now in jeopardy. In hot pursuit of an ideological victory, a handful of extremists at the White House and the Agency for International Development (A.I.D.) aim to destroy America's international family planning program - and Planned Parenthood in particular.
>
> Their motive? Unable to impose their fanatical anti-family planning agenda on the American people they have decided to victimize people who can't fight back.
>
> It looks like an easy win to them.And the fact is, unless we fight back, hardship and suffering will come to those who rely on us for help.
>
> The very survival of women and children is at stake in this battle. So are the long-term prospects for dozens of developing countries.[91]

The ad is a masterpiece. It totally ignores the main issue of the debate, which is whether American taxpayers should subsidize coercive programmes of birth control. Readers are led to believe that Third World women beat a path to Planned Parenthood's door begging for assistance, whereas in fact, PP and other organisations put enormous pressure on these women to accept programmes they don't want. And when persuasion doesn't work, they applaud coercive measures such as those in China. Food aid is given in such a manner as to force individuals into family planning programmes. The ad claims, "Millions of children have been spared the ravages of hunger," but doesn't say how: they were never allowed to be born. It implies that low birth rates promote economic development, whereas it is economic development that reduces birth rates.[92]

In 1966 India was suffering from massive starvation. Advisers to President Lyndon Johnson suggested that the US ship wheat to India. Johnson "demanded that the Indian government first agree to mount a massive birth control program. The Indians finally moved and Johnson released the wheat over a sufficiently extended period to make certain the birth control program was off the ground."[93]

Through AID and other groups the US government continued to promote this agenda. Some programmes achieved their goals through the cynical manipulation of greed and peer pressure. Entire villages, for example, were promised food or money in exchange for "persuading" child-bearing couples to stop having children.

> In one case, villagers in India were offered cash payments on condition that 75 percent of all men in the village submit to vasectomy; and in another Indian village, '100 percent of the eligible couples' accepted family planning, mostly vasectomy, in exchange for a new village well. Though the next step, the compulsory sterilization campaign, gave Indian family planning a rather bad press, with 3 million sterilized within six months in 1976 over the protests of numerous killed or wounded, the principle of 'motivation' stands unchallenged in foreign aid circles.[94]

In Indonesia, AID programmes gave bonuses to individuals for "recruiting" clients for contraceptive services. Villages were assigned quotas and if these quotas were met the entire village was rewarded with food, health services or other benefits.[95] Kasun says that the "foreign aid establishment" prefers this system of group incentives "because they avoid the appearance of paying individuals to use birth control or to have themselves sterilized." She writes, "The woman who volunteers for IUD insertion in Indonesia will not only enjoy the village's food bonus but will earn her neighbors' gratitude for their share of the booty. Conversely, those who refuse this 'service' will be depriving their neighbors as well as themselves of food."[96]

In some cases the methods used in Indonesia were less subtle. Harvard Professor Donald P. Warwick says, "In the presence of civilian, military, and police leaders, women were taken to a house in which IUDs were being inserted. They were asked to go in one door and put under very strong pressure to accept an IUD before they could leave by another door. Whether this was coercion or heavy persuasion, it denied voluntary choice to acceptors..."[97]

But what is behind all this preoccupation with "overpopulation"? Is it really concern for the welfare of the world's people? We have already seen that the population fear-mongers point to India, China, Africa and Pakistan while ignoring New Jersey and England. In a fund-raising letter Planned Parenthood said:

> Thai women and millions of other women like them in India, China, Africa and throughout the developing nations control our destiny. Their decisions – decisions of hundreds of millions of young women – about their family's size – control your future more securely, more relentlessly than the oil crisis or the nuclear arms race.
> ...unless population growth is harnessed and slowed to meet the limited resources and human services of these nations, development of nations will be shattered. Chaos, mass famine and war will continue to increase. We will be affected for better or worse.[98]

Notice the fear-mongering of this letter. It tells its predominantly white readers that women in India, China and Africa control their destinies, and that these women cause "chaos, mass famine and war". There is no reference to the child-bearing women or high population density of any white country. It appears that overpopulation is a term used to describe countries inhabited by non-whites only. Thomas Sowell notes the selective use of the "overpopulation" accusation as well. He points out, "It should be noted, first of all, that *rich* people are never called 'teeming masses,' no matter how many of them there are per square mile. Wealthy Park Avenue neighborhoods have concentrations of people that will compare with slums around the world."[99] Perhaps "overpopulation" is the chic form that racism takes amongst white liberals. In the guise of concern, and in the name of environmentalism, white leftists can advocate coercive population control of blacks in Africa or of Asians in Thailand.

Eugenics and Population Control

This is not a coincidence. In the early 1900s a movement spread across the world to promote "scientific" breeding of people. Called eugenics, this movement was influential in all the major Western nations. Much concern was voiced about how the "unfit" over-reproduce. And, of course, the "unfit" were usually non-white (though some whites *were* deemed "unfit", usually Catholics in a Protestant country or the poor).

In 1912 the movement held the First International Congress of Eugenics. The purpose of the meeting was "the prevention of the propagation of the unfit".[100] Vice-presidents of the conference included Winston Churchill; the president of Stanford University, David Starr Jordan; and the president emeritus of Harvard University, Charles Elliot. The major debate in the eugenics movement was not *whether* people should be sterilized but *who* should be sterilised. Eugenicists in the USA persuaded many state governments to pass laws forcing "unfit" individuals to be sterilised. The state of Indiana passed a law allowing the sterilisation of the mentally handicapped in 1907. Within six years ten other states followed suit.[101] By 1924 these laws had lead to the sterilisation of almost 6000 people.[102] Almost all of them were poor or black. Compulsory sterilisation was on statute books across the United States before it was introduced by the Nazis in Germany.

The American eugenics movement attracted a great deal of attention in Germany and helped legitimise Hitler's theories. Hitler himself praised the efforts of these advocates of "racial" purity. In *Mein Kampf* he lamented that individuals could be full citizens of a country without passing the necessary racial qualifications. The only bright spot that Hitler could find was the United States. He said:

> At present there exists one State which manifests at least some modest attempts that show a better appreciation of how things ought to be done in this matter. It is not, however, in our model German Republic but in the U.S.A. that efforts are made to conform at least partly to the counsels of commonsense. By refusing immigrants to enter there if they are in a bad state of health, and by excluding certain races from the right to become naturalized as citizens, they have begun to introduce principles similar to those on which we wish to group the People's State.[103]

In 1935 an International Congress for Population Science was held in Berlin. The senior American delegate, Clarence G. Campbell, declared that Hitler had built his race policies on the ideas of eugenicists from around the world. The Nazi programme, he said, was "a comprehensive race policy of population development and improvement that promises to be epochal in racial history." These policies set "the pattern which other nations and other racial groups must follow, if they do not wish to fall behind in their racial quality, in their racial accomplishment, and in their prospect of survival."[104]

Eugenic News, a major American publication of the population control movement, said in 1934:

> One may condemn the Nazi policy generally, but specifically it remained for Germany in 1933 to lead the great nations of the world in the recognition of the biological foundations for national character. It is probable that the sterilization statutes of the several American states and the national sterilization statute of Germany will, in legal history, constitute a milestone which marks the control by the most advanced nations of the world of a major aspect of controlling human reproduction, comparable in importance only with the states' legal control of marriage.[105]

In 1935, Leon F. Whitney, secretary of the American Eugenics

Society, expressed his support for the race policies of Hitler. "Many far-sighted men and women in both England and America have long been working earnestly toward something very like what Hitler has now made compulsory."[106] Eugenicist William W. Peter, secretary for the American Public Health Association, argued that Germany needed to follow radical measures to control the racial purity of the nation. Peter argued that the Germans were forced to "depend more than ever upon their own resources" but that "these resources are much depleted." The conclusion was "the present load of social irresponsibles are liabilities which represent a great deal of waste."[107]

Harry Laughlin, another prominent eugenicist, was so impressed with Nazi efforts that he purchased an English version of a Nazi propaganda film on sterilisation. The film, produced by the Racial Political Office of the Nazi Party, was bought for a screening at the Carnegie Institution but later Laughlin raised money to have it edited for wider distribution. The film was retitled *Eugenics in Germany* and was widely promoted by the Eugenics Research Association and the Pioneer Fund.[108] The latter group continues to this day spending millions of dollars to promoted eugenics and population control.

American support for Hitler and his population policies was not limited to verbal praise."The Rockefeller Foundation played a central role in establishing and sponsoring major eugenic institutes in Germany, including the Kaiser Wilhelm Institute for Psychiatry and the Kaiser Wilhelm Institute for Anthropology, Eugenics, and Human Heredity."[109]

Support continued even after the German eugenics movements and these institutions were controlled by the Nazis. The Rockefeller Foundation to this day is a major funder of efforts to control population growth in Third World countries. The rhetoric, of course, has changed somewhat since the 1930s: it wouldn't be acceptable in "liberal" societies today to refer to non-whites as unfit. Instead, the literature focuses on environmental issues. But there is a direct connection between the population control movement of today and the eugenics movement of yesterday. In fact, it was within the eugenics movement that the modern population control organisations were born. Some of the most prominent advocates of birth control, like the sainted Margaret Sanger, were also very active in promoting eugenics. In her magazine, *Birth Control Review,* Sanger wrote in 1919, "More children from the fit, less from the unfit—that is the child issue of birth control."[110] Sanger founded the American Birth Control League, which became the Birth Control Federation, which is the parent of Planned Parenthood. Sanger opened the pages of her publication to prominent Nazis like Ernst Rüdin who helped formulate German racial policies. His article in *Birth Control Review* called for state action to "prevent the multiplication of bad stocks" and "increase the birth-rate of the sound average population".[111] Others, like the Population Reference Bureau of Guy Irving Burch, continue to operate today. Burch, in 1945, called for the compulsory sterilisation of "all persons who are inadequate, either biologically or socially."[112] It is the PRB that takes credit for inventing the term "population bomb".

These are some of the organisations that are used by AID to wage the war on population in the Third World. For political reasons the US government does not directly finance coercive sterilisation or other Third World birth control programmes. Instead, it channels funds to population groups in the States, which then transfer the money to the less savory programmes in the non-white nations. AID also gives "money to international 'private' organizations such as the International Planned Parenthood Foundation (IPPF) and UNFPA and has them do the job."[113] In 1977 an Irish newspaper reported a speech in which a top AID official "has said the U.S. is seeking to provide the means to sterilize a quarter of all Third World women..."[114]

The process for implementing this plan has been described by Julian Simon:

First, U.S. national policy as executed by AID aims to induce *all* people in other countries to use contraceptives whether or not they initially wish to. Second, in 1969-70 AID was able to exert pressure on U.S. universities, private U.S. foundations, and international organizations to move "toward greater activism." This move was facilitated by the sudden big-bang join-up of population activists and environmentalists. Third, in order to avoid charges of interfering with foreign governments, AID gives U.S. taxpayers' money to private organizations to persuade foreign governments to alter their population policies. AID was not merely trying to help other countries achieve their own aims, but was (and still is) trying to pressure foreign governments to do what the U.S. population activists want to see done abroad.[115]

Margaret Wolfson of the Organization for Economic Co-operation and Development discussed how AID would use intermediary organisations to channel money into projects that were politically sensitive:

...the relationship that has developed between Pathfinder [a private population control organisation] and AID works well and is to the advantage of both parties. AID, which has always made extensive use of intermediary nongovernmental bodies in all sectors of its development programme, finds that in the field of population assistance, Pathfinder, with its close and varied contact in developing countries, offers possibilities for action that it would often be difficult for it to take itself, operation on a direct government-to-government basis.[116]

Even a commission of the US government, the Commission on the Organization of the Government for the Conduct of Foreign Policy, admitted that racism motivated many supporters of birth control for the Third World: "Rapid population growth occurs in nonwhite societies, and its continuation represents a threat to values inherent in western civilization as we know it. Nonwhite populations are less desirable because they are less capable and less productive..." The Commission said that this type of thinking motivated "key members of the Congress responsible for foreign aid authorization and appropriations, and some of the private citizens who have been associated with activities to curb rapid population growth."[117]

Simon contends that the same factors that motivate birth control programmes around the world also motivate the policies of the birth control movement in the United States. For example, birth control clinics are disproportionately placed in black residential areas:

> We can also learn about mixed motives from domestic experience with birth-control programs. The date of opening state-supported birth-control clinics was closely related to the concentrations of poor black people in various states. As of 1965, 79 percent of the state-supported clinics in the United States were in the ten states of Alabama, Arkansas, Florida, Georgia, Kentucky, Mississippi, North Carolina, South Carolina, Tennessee, and Virginia, which have only 19 percent of the country's population. Analysis that allows for per capita income shows that the proportion of blacks in a local population is closely related to the density of family planning clinics.
>
> Can one be surprised that many white people in the United States want there to be fewer black people in the world? In sad truth, it is no more surprising than Hindus in India and Christians in Lebanon fearing a high Moslem birthrate, blacks in Uganda tossing out Indians, and so on throughout the world. But in this age when prejudice is not publicly acceptable, racist acts are justified on the basis of supposed economic, political, sociological, and environmental considerations.[118]

Thomas Littlewood hit the nail on the head when he said that in population politics, "humanitarian and bigot can find room under the same tent."[119]

5 THE SHAMBLES OF AFRICA

Throughout the world living standards are improving, birth rates are falling and population growth is steadily coming to a halt–with one exception: Africa. In spite of foreign aid, or perhaps partly because of it, African countries are, in general, forced to make do with less and less food each year while their populations continue to expand. Whereas the Total Fertility Rate in South America dropped from 6.4 to 4.1 from 1950-55 to 1980-85, Africa's TFR remained almost stagnant over the same period, dropping only from 6.5 to 6.4. By 1995 it dropped again but only to 5.8.

But given that birth rates fall as economies grow, this is to be expected. Africa is the last continent on the planet where economic disasters are commonplace. With the collapse of socialism in Eastern Europe, even those countries are finally experiencing growth, but Africa, as a whole, continues to follow outmoded concepts of socialist planning and state control.

People often argue that countries are poor because they have too many people and not enough resources. But this just doesn't hold for Africa. The fact is that Africa is less densely populated than many of the wealthy countries of the world. With a land mass three times larger than the United States, for example, it has only twice the population.

Lord Bauer, in *The Development Frontier,* suggests that the *lack* of people in Africa may be the cause of some of the problems:

> ...population growth can have favorable external effects. It can facilitate the more effective division of labor and thereby increase real incomes. In fact, in much of Southeast Asia, Africa, and Latin America, **sparseness of population inhibits economic advance.** It retards the development of transport facilities and communications, and thus inhibits the movement of people and goods and the spread of new ideas and methods. These obstacles to enterprise and economic advance are particularly difficult to overcome.[120]

Bauer isn't alone in making this observation. A growing number of "authorities believe that Africa is actually *underpopulated.* Africa is now the world's most sparsely populated continent (although it now has the most rapid population growth rate) and many parts of it are so sparsely populated that it is unable to support anything more than very rudimentary communications and transportation networks. The result is that the distribution and diffusion of goods, services, and ideas are severely retarded."[121] The sparse population of Africa may be contributing to its economic malaise, but as we shall see it is not the main factor.

As for the second part of the argument – that Africa is poor because there are "not enough resources" – we know that some of the most developed countries in the world (e.g. Singapore, Hong Kong and Switzerland) are not blessed with natural resources. And Africa is one of the richest continents in the world. It is abundantly endowed with natural resources which for the most part are misused, unused or squandered by corrupt governments. David Lamb notes that Africa

> has 40 percent of the world's potential hydroelectric power supply; the bulk of the world's gold; 90 percent of its cobalt; 50 percent of its phosphates; 40 percent of its platinum; 7.5 percent of its coal; 8 percent of its known petroleum reserves; 12 percent of its natural gas; 3 percent of its iron ores;

Population density per square mile
European versus African countries

Monaco	38,666	Rwanda (pre-94)	747
Vatican City	6,666	Burundi	526
San Marino	958	Nigeria	333
Netherlands	919	Gambia	204
Belgium	840	Malawi	199
United Kingdom	606	Uganda	192
Germany	563	Ghana	166
Italy	496	Togo	163
Liechtenstein	484	Lesotho	150
Switzerland	415	Sierre Leone	150
Luxembourg	370	Morocco	148
Poland	318	Egypt	142
Czechoslovakia	318	Tunisia	128
Denmark	309	Swaziland	116
Portugal	296	Kenya	113
Albania	295	Senegal	102
Hungary	294	Ethiopia	101
Andorra	282	Ivory Coast	97
France	267	Burkina Faso	85
Romania	254	South Africa	84
Yugoslavia	254	Guinea	77
Austria	244	Tanzania	71
Bulgaria	234	Zimbabwe	68
Spain	203	Guinea-Bissau	67
Greece	198	Liberia	62
Ireland	198	Cameroon	60
Sweden	48	Madagascar	52
Finland	38	Mozambique	48
Norway	28	Zaire	39

Additional African countries: Djibouti, 38; Somalia, 34; Equatorial Guinea, 31; Zambia, 28; Sudan, 26; Angola, 20; Mali, 19; Congo, 17; Niger, 17; Central African Republic, 12; Gabon, 12; Benin,11; Chad, 10; Libya, 6; Botswana, 5; Mauritania, 5; and Namibia, 4.

and millions upon millions of acres of untilled farmland. There is not another continent blessed with such abundance.[122]

As far as food production is concerned, Africa's potential is staggering. Unfortunately, the reality is depressing. During the 1930s Africa was a food exporter. In the 1950s it was still self-sufficient. But with independence came a major decline in food production. D. Gale Johnson points out:

> Africa had a constant average level of per capita food production during the 1950s and 1960s and a shocking decline during the 1970s. In 1980 per capita food production in Africa (excluding South Africa) was 15 percent below 1969-71. Total food production increased 10 percent while population grew by about 25 percent, resulting in an unprecedented decline in per capita food production. The decline in per capita food production was not due to a lack of resources but to many factors that were primarily political in nature – the exploitation of farmers through low prices, civil unrest, military conflict and the creation of millions of refugees.[123]

The decline in African food production has been astonishing. For instance, Mozambique produced 216,000 tons of cashew nuts in 1972 but only 1,000 in 1985; sugar production fell from 285,581 tons in 1974 to just 120,000 tons in 1982; maize production declined from 400,000 tons in 1972 to 200,000 by 1983; rice dropped from 111,000 tons in 1972 to 30,000 tons in 1983; and bananas fell from 280,000 tons in 1972 to just 73,000 tons in 1983.[124]

Ethiopia offers another example of a richly endowed country destroyed by socialist policies and corrupt government. The *New York Times* once said that Ethiopia "could easily become the breadbasket for much of Europe if her agriculture were better organized."[125] Agronomist Doreen Warriner wrote, "Ethiopia is one of those rare countries so richly endowed by nature that the agrarian structure, feudal in every sense of the term, does appear to be the only constraint on development."[126] Ethiopia did abandon its feudal system in 1974

– not for capitalism, however, but for a radical brand of communism under Marxist Mengistu Haile Mariam. The new government rapidly turned Ethiopia into a basket case, not a breadbasket.

Thousands were killed by the government, including Emperor Haile Selassie and many of his family, and more than 30,000 were jailed. Peasant farmers were uprooted from their land in one of the most massive relocation programmes the world has known: an estimated 75 percent of the populace was forcibly moved. One Ethiopian bureaucrat announced, "It is our duty to move the peasants if they are too stupid to move by themselves." Land was nationalised in the name of the people, and food production plummeted. Famine quickly appeared and the capitalist West poured food relief into the country, but Mengistu simply used the food as a political weapon, allowing tens of thousands of people to starve to death. While the country was in the grip of famine, Mengistu spent almost $200 million celebrating the tenth anniversary of socialism in the country. Caviar and champagne, lobster and salmon were imported for the Marxist elite to consume, and $10 million was spent just to refurbish the statues of Marx, Lenin and Engels that decorated the streets of Addis Ababa. When the people finally had enough and overthrew Mengistu, he fled to Mugabe's Zimbabwe where he was welcomed with open arms.[127]

Tanzania also destroyed free markets in favour of state control and socialism, with similar results. The problems in Tanzania began when president Julius Nyerere issued the Arusha Declaration, a plan for turning the country into a socialist paradise. The major industries were socialised and massive resettlement programmes were forced on the people. The old villages were destroyed and the peasant farmers forced into collectives. Government regulations required that food be sold to the government. Again, food production plummeted and people could no longer find enough to eat.[128] Swedish economist Sven Rydenfelt tells what happened:

By 1979, five years after the enforced resettlement, domestic agricultural production in Tanzania was already incapable of providing the cities with food. Imports had to be increased to compensate for declining production, and in 1980 no less than half of the food needed by Tanzania was being imported. A decade of socialist agricultural policy had been sufficient to destroy the socio-ecological system.[129]

Rydenfelt quotes a Norwegian newspaper that reported, "Large sectors of the production system stand still, food lines in the capital city of Dar es Salaam were never longer, and shop shelves never more empty."[130] According to World Bank statistics the Tanzanian economy contracted on average 0.5% each year between 1965 and 1988, and personal consumption dropped by 43%.[131] A Norwegian radio commentator who visited Tanzania in 1982 reported:

> On days when bread was delivered to the stores, people had to line up for hours. Even commodities like soap, toothpaste, salt, flour, cooking oil, batteries and bandages were lacking. People starve, and starving people get desperate... The brutal truth is that the policy of President Nyerere has completely failed... The Tanzanians are unable to manage the many state enterprises, and today production is only 30 percent of its volume a few years ago.[132]

In Ghana, the same story was repeated. President Nkrumah announced that he would rule the country with "African socialism". Ghana was doing well in 1960, largely because of its cocoa production; that year it produced 439,000 tons of cocoa. The government saw this as a gold mine and decreed that all cocoa must be sold to a government marketing board at prices well below world prices. The results weren't felt immediately–they rarely are. In fact, cocoa production increased to 581,000 tons in 1964, but then the effects of the policies kicked in. By 1970 production was down to 406,000 tons, by 1978 to 270,000 tons and in 1982 to 225,000 tons. In other words, the socialist price controls and marketing board had managed to destroy over half of Ghana's cocoa production in just two decades.[133]

The state farms created by Nkrumah were predictably a failure. Ghanaian economist George Ayittey writes:

> In 1965 the state farms barely produced enough food to feed their own workers, let alone the nation. After only three years of operation these government farms had accumulated losses of over $15 million. Between 1960 and 1966 local food prices doubled as a result of these shortages. The reaction of the Nkrumah government to rising food prices was one of paranoia. Instead of acknowledging the shortfalls in food production, Nkrumah blamed neocolonialist agents and economic saboteurs.[134]

Ayittey notes that instead of learning from Nkrumah's failure "one country after another, with deadly consistency, followed in his footsteps: Guinea, Mali, Congo-Brazzaville, Tanzania, Zambia, and a host of others."[135] The results everywhere were the same: "in each country tyranny followed, economies were ruined, and the nationalists were ousted by the military. Incredibly, 25 years after the failure of Nkrumah's socialist experiment, Zimbabwe was charging obstinately along the same disastrous lines."[136]

While the governments of Africa have ploughed along the socialist path, the people have seen their incomes deteriorate and their once-productive nations become centres of starvation. Average incomes have been declining: "...the countries of sub-Saharan Africa (excluding South Africa) have an average per capita income of only $210. And while Africa is the only continent in which incomes have declined, averaging a 0.1 percent decline per year for the last two decades, what is most alarming is that the rate of decline has been accelerating."[137]

But the failure of Africa is the failure of socialism, not the failure of Africans. The same policies in Russia and China led to similar results. That is why both nations have abandoned socialism and moved toward capitalism. *Ecocide*, a book exposing the environmental disasters of state socialism, noted that the food crisis that continually dogged the Soviet Union was not caused by bad farmers. "Soviets can farm well. On their private plots–just 1 or 2 percent of all land – they produced 'about two-thirds of the potatoes and eggs and about 40 percent of meat, milk and vegetables' consumed in the mid-1960s. On those tiny patches of ground, they worked for themselves – hard and productively. On the huge holdings of the state and collective farms, their performance was miserable, even dangerous."[138]

David Osterfeld says that the results of African socialism were predictable:

> Not only were they what one would expect from elementary economic theory: they were also what one could observe after a half century of experience with socialism in the Second World. The (former) Soviet Union contains some of the most fertile agricultural land in the world. Prior to the communist revolution in 1917, Russia was the world's largest exporter of grain. Collectivization of agriculture during the 1920s and 1930s was quickly followed by dramatic declines in output. Between 5 and 10 million Russians died of starvation during these years, with 12 to 13 million more saved by food donated by the Western capitalist countries. By the 1980s the Soviet Union employed 25 percent of its labor force and invested in excess of 25 percent of its capital in agriculture, both figures far higher than in any other industrialized country. Despite its tremendous agricultural potential, the Soviet Union became the world's largest food importer. It imported nearly one-third of its food, and this is despite having grudgingly permitted the establishment of private minifarms one-half to one acre in size. These private plots made up only 3 percent of the total cropland, yet produced 27 percent of the nation's food.
>
> ....The pattern is repeated with monotonous regularity throughout socialist countries. Most of the Eastern European countries are blessed with fertile agricultural land and, prior to socialism, were food exporters. The adoption of socialist policies in most of these was quickly followed by declining production, food shortages, and bread lines. Zinsmeister notes that "between 1960 and 1980 agricultural productivity declined by one-third in the Soviet Bloc."
>
> Agricultural output in China was virtually stagnant during the 25-year reign of Mao Tse-tung. The Chinese government now acknowledges that during just one three-year period, the so-called Three Difficult Years from 1959-1962, between 25 and 30 million Chinese died from starvation. By the time of Mao's death in the mid 1970s, the average Chinese was less well fed

than he was during the 1920s or even during the Japanese occupation of the 1930s. Beginning in 1977, Mao's successors abandoned his "socialist experiment." As a result, says *The Economist,* "food grain output has increased by 12% a year since then, despite bad weather in 1980."[139]

In 1989 Yury Chernichenko, a member of the Soviet Union's Congress of People's Deputies, told the assembly, "A coercive system of farming will never feed the people."[140] That is a lesson many countries in Africa have yet to learn.

Apartheid and Overpopulation

For 45 years South African politics has been totally dominated by the issue of apartheid. Opponents of apartheid used every means possible to discredit and destroy the system, and that is perfectly understandable. As a result, however, apartheid has been blamed for many social ills that it had nothing to do with creating. For example, Barbara Klugman, an anthropologist at the University of the Witwatersrand, oversteps the facts when she attempts to prove that "overpopulation" in South Africa is a result of apartheid. To be fair, she does not argue that apartheid is *entirely* responsible; she believes some of the blame must be laid at the door of the developed nations of the world. She vigorously defends the people of Africa from the charge that poverty is the result of high birth rates. As noted earlier, this is one area where I agree with her.

To Klugman, the overpopulation issue is one of colonial exploitation and apartheid. Third World countries are poor because First World countries are rich. There is no mutually beneficial trade in her analysis. Trade is exploitation. She says:

> ...the relative wealth of the First World derives directly from its use of Third World resources and Third World markets on terms of trade which have

always been advantageous to the First World. It is incorrect to see the wealth of the First World, and the poverty of the Third World, as simple facts which bear no relation to each other.[141]

Lord Bauer has debunked this myth quite thoroughly. He points out that the countries of the developed world were wealthy compared to so-called Third World nations long before they ever had contact with each other. First World wealth did not depend on Third World resources in the past, nor does it do so today. Various studies have shown that colonialism tended to be economically unprofitable for the colonial powers and that they spent more money on the colonies than they earned from them. In fact, contrary to Klugman's theory, the more trade Third World countries have with First World nations, the wealthier they become. If First World wealth is created by taking advantage of Third World nations, then those Third World nations with the least amount of international trade should be the wealthiest: Hong Kong and Singapore should be sinking into poverty whereas Zimbabwe and Cuba should be economic miracles. In the real world, of course, the facts are completely the reverse. Those Third World countries that have high economic growth and prosperity are also those countries that have the greatest amount of trade with the First World.

Klugman is a fervent critic of apartheid and it is a fairly safe bet that she supported trade sanctions against South Africa. Yet, according to her own theory, sanctions should have increased South Africa's wealth. If the First World exploits its Third World trading partners, then the greater the trade South Africa had with the First World the less capable the South African government would have been of implementing apartheid.

Like others on the left, Klugman sees overpopulation as a problem of resource *distribution*, not of resource *production*. Typically, the solution they offer is to confiscate the wealth of the First World and redistribute it, not to promote economic policies that would enable

Third World countries to become prosperous and self-sufficient. According to their analysis, the crisis in Ethiopia should not be laid at the door of the Ethiopian Marxists who destroyed that nation: the real criminals are the wealthy people in North America and Europe who consume too much. The fact that Africa was once able to feed itself (under the evil colonialists that Klugman despises) is irrelevant: the poverty/overpopulation problem is not caused by some people having too little but by others having too much.

Klugman writes: "The argument that the poor of the Third World use proportionately more of the world's resources, while contributing less to the world's GDP, compounds the victim-blaming syndrome. People in the First World consume more resources than those in the Third World...."[142] But that is not the point. The problem that Third World nations face is not how much they consume but the fact that they are not able to produce a surplus. The First World is wealthy because it produces more than it consumes, thus allowing the accumulation of capital and other resources. The Third World is poor because it produces barely enough to survive, and sometimes not even that. What the wealthy and the poor consume relative to each other is unimportant. What is crucial is what each produces relative to what they, themselves, consume.

What role did apartheid play in causing "overpopulation" in South Africa, according to Klugman? She simply asserts that apartheid laws "upset the balance between population and resources, and hence between population and the environment. Not only has it created massive inequalities in the use of resources, but it has also resulted in a high population growth rate."[143] Does this argument make sense? If high population growth rates are caused by apartheid, then why are there high population growth rates in the rest of Africa where there is no apartheid? Why did England experience a soaring population growth rate during the industrial revolution? Why have there been high growth rates in virtually every poverty-stricken nation in the world when they first began to develop economically? The coloureds in South Africa were surely victims of apartheid as well, yet their population growth rate is almost identical to that of South African whites.

Klugman errs in equating high population density with overpopulation. Early in her essay she shows that countries with high population densities are not necessarily overpopulated. But then she says, "There is overcrowding because people have been forced into the 'homelands' instead of being allowed to remain on the land on which they were born or move to urban areas."[144] Now, of course, overpopulation and population density are not the same thing. Most African poverty is found in the less densely populated rural areas, not in areas of high population density like Hillbrow in Johannesburg. Africans continue to flood into Hillbrow because they have a better chance of improving their living standards. As I have pointed out earlier, high population density has certain economic advantages and that is true in South Africa as well. Apartheid in fact attempted to prevent blacks from moving from the less populated rural areas to the more densely populated cities.

Finally, Klugman attempts to debunk the claim that high population growth rates in South Africa are the result of lower mortality rates: "The other misconception held by the overpopulation theorists is that the population growth rate among Africans is high because the mortality rate has dropped through access to modern medicine."[143] The way Klugman attempts to disprove this theory is to point out that black South Africans don't have the same access to medicine as do white South Africans. Again, she misses the point. What is relevant here is how much access black Africans have to medicine today compared to 20 years ago or 100 years ago. While black South Africans do not have the same access to medical care as whites, they have more access today than they did a hundred years ago, and mortality rates have declined. The average life expectancy in Africa for blacks has increased dramatically over the last 50 years. Africans today have more access to modern medicine than at any time in history and as a result they are living longer. Since birth rates in Africa have remained steady, the increase in population density should be expected.

In her attempt to blame apartheid for overpopulation and poverty Klugman distorts reality. "It is not population numbers that threaten South Africa, but the lack of access to resources on the one hand and overconsumption of resources on the other. It is not the poor themselves who have caused their poverty, by having many children, but the practice of discrimination...."[146]

The causes of poverty are complex. Certainly discrimination alone is not sufficient to cause poverty, as the Jews and the Chinese have proved the world over. Moreover, the high population growth rates South Africa is experiencing are not at all unique – they have been experienced all over the world by many different societies, including all the nations currently deemed to be First World.

More importantly, the solution to these problems requires more than the dismantling of apartheid. A more equitable "distribution" of resources (i.e. socialist redistributive policies) is not the way to solve South Africa's, or the world's, remaining "overpopulation" problem. As we have seen, everywhere socialism has been tried, the problem grew worse because food production and resource recovery suffered severely. To solve its problems, South Africa must deregulate its heavily regulated economy and increase its trade with the First World. Instead of simply redistributing the relatively little wealth that already exists, South Africa needs a growing economy that creates new wealth. The only method yet discovered to do that is through the forces of a relatively free market with private property.

Conclusion

This paper has tackled some rather difficult issues – difficult not because the evidence is lacking for the ideas it has presented, but because the ideas run contrary to much modern mythology. It has shown that the world is not overpopulated in any meaningful sense of the word, that food production per capita is increasing and that there is plenty of room for all of us, and more than enough natural resources to meet our needs for thousands of years to come.

Overpopulation is blamed for hunger and famine everywhere, particularly in Africa. But, as this paper has shown, Africa is the least populated of all the continents and has the ability to feed the entire world two times over. Yet still Africa is impoverished. A continent blessed with abundant resources and capable of feeding the world is starving. Poverty is so commonplace that it is expected. A scapegoat must be found. The accepted theory is that it is the fault of the Africans themselves. They reproduce too quickly and that is why they are starving. It is a classic case of blaming the victim.

The people of Africa are the victims of inept governments that have attempted to impose socialism and regulated economies on countries that can't afford these wealth-destroying policies. They deserve better than this.

The good news for the people of Africa is that they need not suffer in poverty any longer. The solution is simple: free the people to produce; allow the people to keep what they produce; and the people will produce.

FOOTNOTES

1. *Wall Street Journal,* 30 October 1985.

2. Paddock, William and Paul, *Famine—1975!* (Boston: Little, Brown, 1967), p 222.

3. Simon, Julian, *Population Matters* (New Jersey: Transaction Publications, 1990), pp 364-365.

4. *Ibid,* p 103.

5. "World is nearing limit to provide food: Report", *The Citizen,* Johannesburg, 17 January 1994, p 16.

6. *Ibid.*

7. *Ibid.*

8. Bailey, Ronald, *Eco-Scam* (New York: St. Martin's Press, 1993), p 46.

9. *Ibid.*

10. Kasun, Jacqueline, *The War Against Population* (San Francisco: Ignatius, 1988), p 21.

11. *Ibid.*

12. Burts, John J., and Meeks, Linda Brower, *Education for Sexuality* (Philadelphia: WB Saunders, 1975), p 408.

13. Nisbet, Robert, *History of the Idea of Progress* (New York: Basic Books, 1980), p 52.

14. Jerome, *The Principal Works,* cited in Vinter, Jacob, *Religious Thought and Economic Society* (Durham: Duke University Press, 1978), p 34.

15. Osterfeld, David, *Prosperity Versus Planning* (New York: Oxford University Press, 1992), p 63.

16. Kasun, *The War Against Population,* p 33.

17. Fabricius, Peter, "Too many mouths point to food crisis inside 40 years", *Johannesburg Star,* 16 August 1994, p 9.

18. Simon, Julian, *The Ultimate Resource* (Princeton: Princeton

University Press, 1981), p 64.

19. Simon, Julian, "The State of World Food Supplies", The Atlantic Monthly, July 1981, pp 72-76.

20. Osterfeld, *Planning Versus Prosperity,* p 64.

21. Kasun, *The War Against Population,* p 34.

22. *Ibid,* p 35.

23. Clark, Colin, *Population Growth: The Advantages* (Santa Ana: RL Sassone, 1972), p 44.

24. Maddox, Bronwen, "Too many people, so few resources", *Sunday Times Business Times,* 28 August 1994, p 5.

25. Sowell, Thomas, *Knowledge & Decisions* (New York: Basic Books, 1980), pp 45-46.

26. Page, William, "The Non-Renewable Resources Sub-System," in HSD Coles et al, *Models of Doom: A Critique of the Limits to Growth* (New York: Universe Books, 1973), p 36.

27. Simon, *The Ultimate Resource,* p 17.

28. Sowell, *Knowledge & Decisions,* pp 167-168.

29. Kahn, Herman, *The Next 200 Years* (London: Abacus, 1977), p 102.

30. *Ibid.*

31. Meadows, Donella et al, *The Limits of Growth: A Report for the Club of Rome's Project on the Predicament of Mankind* (New York: New American Library, 1972), pp 64-67.

32. Taylor, Gordon Rattray, *The Doomsday Book* (London: Thames and Hudson, Ltd., 1970), p 292.

33. *Ibid.* p 208.

34. Osterfeld, *Prosperity Versus Planning,* p 86.

35. *Ibid.*

36. Simon, *Population Matters,* p 90.

37. Osterfeld, *Prosperity Versus Planning,* pp 85-86.

38. Page, William, in *Models of Doom: A Critique of the Limits to Growth* , p 38.

39. Bailey, Ronald, *Eco-Scam* (New York: St. Martin's Press, 1993), p 67.

40. Julian Simon, *Population Matters,* p 369.

41. *Ibid,* pp 365-366.

42. *Ibid,* pp 371-372.

43. Bailey, *Eco-Scam,* pp 53-54.

44. Kahn, *The Next 200 Years,* p 90.

45. Quoted in Simon, *The Ultimate Resource,* p 35.

46. Quoted in Walter, Edward, *The Immorality of Limiting Growth* (Albany: State University of New York Press, 1981), p 131.

47. Singer, Max, "The Serious Errors Inherent in a Doomsday View" in *Rational Readings on Environmental Concerns* (New York: Van Nostrand Reinhold, 1992) p 701.

48. Bailey, *Eco-Scam,* p 51.

49. *Ibid.*

50. Taylor, *The Doomsday Book,* pp 222-228.

51. *Ibid,*p 229.

52. *Ibid,* p 230.

53. Julian Simon, *The Ultimate Resource,* p 255.

54. Bloch, Ben and Lyons, Harold, *Apocalypse Not* (Washington, D.C.: Cato Institute, 1993), pp 26-27.

55. Sowell, Thomas, *The Economics and Politics of Race* (William Morrow & Company, New York, 1983) pp 211-212.

56. For further research on the non-threat of global warming I suggest, Michaels, Patrick, *Sound and Fury: The Science and Politics of Global Warming* (Washington DC; Cato Institute, 1992), Balling Jr., Robert, *The Heated Debate* (San Francisco: Pacific Research Institute for Public Policy, 1992); Singer, Fred S, *Global Climate Change* (New York: Paragon Press, 1989).

57. Keyfitz, Nathan, "The Growing Human Population" in *Managing the Planet* (WH Freeman and Company, New York, 1990), p 63.

58. *Ibid.*

59. Kasun, *The War Against Population,* p 50.

60. *Ibid.* pp 52, 56.

61. Boserup, Ester, *Population and Technological Change* (Chicago: University of Chicago, 1981), p 129.

62. Kahn, *The Next 200 Years,* p 33.

63. *Ibid.*

64. Osterfeld, *Prosperity Versus Planning,* p 106.

65. "World's population growth slows down", *The Citizen,* Johannesburg, 7 August, 1995, p 17.

66. *Ibid,* pp 108-109.

67. Wattenberg, Ben and Zinsmeister, Karl (eds), *Are Population Trends a Problem?* (Washington DC: American Enterprise Institute, 1986), pp 1-2.

68. *Ibid,* p 109.

69. "World's population growth slows down", *The Citizen,* Johannesburg, 7 August, 1995, p 17.

70. Johnson, D. Gale, "Population, Food and Wellbeing;" Paper No. 90:12, University of Chicago Office of Agriculture Economics Research (July 9, 1990), p 24.

71. *Ibid,* pp 113-114.

72. Quoted in Bauer, Peter, *The Development Frontier* (Cambridge: Harvard University Press, 1991), p 23.

73. Kasun, *The War Against Population,* pp 63-64.

74. Klugman, Barbara, "Victims or Villains?" in *Going Green* (Cape Town: Oxford University Press, 1991), p 76

75. For a more thorough look at the reasons why socialism was not able to function economically see: FA Hayek, (ed), *Collectivist Economic Planning* (London: George Routledge & Sons, 1935); Ludwig von Mises, *Economic Calculation in the Socialist Commonwealth* (Auburn: Ludwig von Mises Institute, 1990); F. A. Hayek, *The Fatal Conceit: the Errors of Socialism* (Chicago: University of Chicago Press, 1988); David Ramsey Steele, *From Marx to Mises* (La Salle: Open Court, 1993); Elisabeth Tamedly, *Socialism and International Economic Order* (Caldwell: Caxton Printers, 1969) and Trygve Hoff, *Economic Calculation in the Socialist Society* (London: William Hodge and Company, 1949).

76. Heilbroner, Robert, "The Triumph of Capitalism," *The New Yorker* (23 January 1989), p 98.

77. Bolch and Lyons, *Apocalypse Not,* p 28.

78. Quoted in Maddox, John, *The Doomsday Syndrome,* p 47.

79. Ehrlich, Paul, *The Population Bomb* (Ballantine; New York, 1968), p xi.

80. Simon, Julian, *The Ultimate Resource,* p 311.

81. *Ibid,* p 315.

82. Irving, David, *The War Path: Hitler's Germany 1933-1939* (Papermac, London, 1985) p 67.

83. Quoted in Eberstadt, Nick, *The Poverty of Communism,* p 117.

84. Wren, Christopher, "Chinese Region Showing Resistance to National Goals for Birth Control", *New York Times,* 16 May 1982.

85. Mosher, Steven, "Why Are Baby Girls Being Killed in China?" *Wall Street Journal,* 25 July 1983.

86. Quoted in Simon, Julian, *Population Matters,* p 231.

87. *Washington Post,* April 10, 1988, p B1.

88. Kasun, Jacquelin, *The War Against Population,* p 90.

89. Eberstadt, Nick, *The Poverty of Communism,* p 117.

90. Quoted in Simon, Julian, *Population Matters,* p 235.

91. *The Washington Post,* 12 March 1987, p A17.

92. The ad also ignored a question that many taxpayers would have liked answered: should a tax-funded organisation be directly involved in a lobbying campaign to affect legislation?

93. Califano, Joseph, *Governing America* (New York: Simon & Schuster, 1981), p 52.

94. Kasun, *The War Against Population,* p 85.

95. *Ibid*, p 84.

96. *Ibid.*

97. Simon, *Population Matters,* p 226.

98. Simon, *The Ultimate Resource,* p 327.

99. Sowell, *The Economics and Politics of Race,* pp 209-210.

100. Kasun, *The War AgainstPopulation,* p 159.

101. Kühl, Stefan, *The Nazi Connection: Eugenics, American Racism, and German National Socialism* (New York: Oxford University Press, 1994), p 17.

102. *Ibid.* p 24.

103. Hitler, Adolph, *Mein Kampf* (London: Hurst and Blackett Ltd., 1939) p 367.

104. Kühl, *The Nazi Connection,* p 34.

105. *Ibid.* p 46.

106. *Ibid.* p 36.

107. *Ibid.* p 55.

108. *Ibid.* p 49.

109. *Ibid.* p 20.

110. Kasun, *The War Against Population,* p 160.

111. *Ibid.*

112. Burch, Guy Irving, and Pendell, Elmer, *Population Roads to Peace or War* (Washington: Population Reference Bureau, 1945), p 103.

113. Simon, *The Ultimate Resource,* p 294.

114. "Population Control of Third World Planned: Sterilisation Storm in U.S.," *Evening Press* (Dublin, Ireland) 12 May 1977, p 9.

115. Simon, *The Ultimate Resource,* p 297.

116. Wolfson, Margaret, *Profiles in Population Assistance,* Development Centre of the Organization for Economic co-operation and Development, 1983, p 173.

117. Simon, *Population Matters,* pp 228-229.

118. *Ibid,* p 229.

119. *Ibid.*

120. Bauer, *The Development Frontier,* p 26.

121. Osterfeld, *Prosperity Versus Planning,* p 128.

122. Lamb, David, *The Africans* (New York: Vantage, 1983), p 20.

123. Johnson, D. Gale, "World Food and Agriculture", in Simon and Kahn, *The Resourceful Earth,* p 73.

124. Caldwell, Don, *South Africa: The New Revolution*

(Johannesburg: FMF Books, 1989), p 219.

125. Osterfeld, *Prosperity Versus Planning,* p 72.

126. Ellis, Gene, "Land Tenancy Reform in Ethiopia", *Economic Development and Cultural Change* (April, 1980), p 526.

127. Ayittey, George, *Africa Betrayed* (New York: St. Martin's Press, 1992), pp 107-108.

128. *Ibid,* p 107.

129. Rydenfelt, Sven, *A Pattern for Failure* (New York: Harcourt, Brace, Jovanovich, 1983), p 121.

130. *Ibid.*

131. Ayittey, *Africa Betrayed,* p 282.

132. Rydenfelt, *A Pattern for Failure,* pp 123-124.

133. *Ibid,* pp 110-111.

134. Ayittey, *Africa Betrayed,* p 168.

135. *Ibid,* p 170.

136. *Ibid.*

137. Osterfeld, *Prosperity Versus Planning,* p.73.

138. Feshbach, Murray and Friendly, Jr., Alfred, *Ecocide in the USSR* (London: Aurum Press, 1992), p 50.

139. Osterfeld, *Prosperity Versus Planning,* p 82. For a more thorough analysis of how communist economics breeds poverty see Nick Eberstadt, *The Poverty of Communism* (New Brunswick: Transaction Books, 1990).

140. Feshbach and Friendly, *Ecocide in the USSR,* p 50.

141. Klugman, in *Going Green,* p 76.

142. *Ibid.*

143. *Ibid,* p 71.

144. *Ibid,* p 73.

145. *Ibid,* p 74.

146. *Ibid,* p 77.

ABOUT THE AUTHOR

Jim Peron is an American writer currently living in Johannesburg, South Africa. He is the coauthor of the book *Liberty Recliamed* with Jim Lewis. He has written for various magazines such as *Reason, Inquiry, Libertarian Review,* and *The Individualist.* He has also written for various newspapers such as *The Oakland Tribune, The Orange County Register, The Hartford Courant, Connecticut Business Times,* and *The San Francisco Business Journal.* He is a former policy analyst for the Pacific Policy Research Institute and worked with the Connecticut Institute where he coauthored a major policy report on the privatisation of highways. He currently works with the Free Market Foundation of Southern Africa which published his last monograph *Affirmative Action, Apartheid and Capitalism.* He may be reached at:

Suite 251
P-Bag X-31
Saxonwold, 2132
South Africa

ABOUT THE FMF

The Free Market Foundation of Southern Africa was established in 1975 to promote the market economy. The FMF sponsors research, publications, conferences, lectures, training programmes and lobbying efforts in support of the free market. Funding comes from membership subscriptions, project sponsorship and income from sales and fees. The most recent Foundation publications are:

South Africa: The New Revolution by Don Caldwell
Liberty and Prosperity: Essays on limiting government and freeing enterprise in South Africa edited by Richard Grant and Frank Vorhies
Privatisation and Economic Justice edited by Frank Vorhies
Consumer Power in a Free Market edited by Terry Markman and Frank Vorhies
South Africa's War Against Capitalism by Walter Williams
The Forgotten Heroes by Ian Hetherington
Nationalisation: How Governments Control You by Richard Grant

The following FMF monographs are also available:
The Fallacy of National Control by Richard Grant
Exchange Controls Must Go by Richard Grant
The Social Market Trap by Christopher Lingle
The Importance of Political Traditions by Leonard Liggio
The Environment: Rights and Freedom by Christopher Lingle
Affirmative Action, Apartheid and Capitalism by Jim Peron
On Industrial Policy by Prof. WD Reekie

THE HEARTLAND INSTITUTE

The Heartland Institute is a nonprofit and nonpartisan source of research and commentary on public policy issues. Its authors specialise in finding market-based solutions to social and economic problems. Its principal audiences are the nation's elected officials, reporters and editors, and other business and community leaders.

Heartland is a genuinely independent source of research and commentary: It is not affiliated with any political party, business, or foundation. It does not accept government funds and does not conduct "contract" research for special interest groups. Its activities are tax-exempt under Section 501(c)3 of the Internal Revenue Code.

Heartland publications have been called "among the premier economic documents being produced anywhere today." In addition to books, policy studies, and shorter commentaries, The Heartland Institute publishes *Intellectual Ammunition,* a bimonthly magazine for state legislators. Heartland also operates a fax-on-demand information service called *PolicyFax,* which provides instant access by telephone and fax to over one thousand documents from nearly one hundred think tanks and publishers.

Further information about The Heartland Institute is available by fax, by calling *PolicyFax* at 510-208-8000. Have your fax machine number ready, and follow the recorded messages. Alternatively, call 708-202-3060 or write: The Heartland Institute, 800 East Northwest Highway, Suite 1080, Palatine, Illinois 60067. Finally, we can be contacted on the Internet through our homepage on the World Wide Web at http://www.heartland.org.

The opinions expressed in this book are those of the author alone. Nothing here should be construed as reflecting the views of The Heartland Institute or as an attempt to aid or hinder the passage of any legislation.